The Ten Commandments and Voting

MomSquad

momsquad.com

The Ten Commandments and Voting

by Remington Comp

MomSquad

momsquad.com

TABLE OF CONTENTS

INTRODUCTION

Introduction — xi
How to Use This Program — xvii

COMMANDMENT 1: THOU SHALT HAVE NO OTHER GODS BEFORE ME — 1

Principle: Center on eternal truth — 1
Precept 1: Both you and your candidates should have a clear moral center based on eternal truth — 4
Precept 2: Some "gods" are not based on eternal truth — 7
Precept 3: Governments exist to secure the "Laws of Nature and of Nature's God" — 9
Proclaim: Who/what are your gods? — 11

COMMANDMENT 2: THOU SHALT NOT MAKE UNTO THEE ANY GRAVEN IMAGE — 15

Principle: Graven images are the tangible manifestations of your gods — 15
Precept 1: Political parties can be graven images — 18
Precept 2: Policies and hot-button issues can be graven images — 21
Proclaim: What are the manifestations of your gods? — 23

TABLE OF CONTENTS

COMMANDMENT 3: THOU SHALT NOT TAKE THE NAME OF THE LORD THY GOD IN VAIN — 27

Principle: The Name of God is I Am — 27

Precept 1 : How someone speaks of themself reflects their gods — 30

Precept 2: How someone speaks of others reflects their gods — 33

Precept 3: The names of graven images reflect who/what your gods are — 36

Precept 4: How you and your candidates treat others in political discourse reflects your gods — 38

Proclaim: What are the names associated with your gods? — 41

COMMANDMENT 4: REMEMBER THE SABBATH DAY TO KEEP IT HOLY — 45

Principle: There is a time set apart to vote, and voting is a sacred responsibility — 45

Precept 1: The process of voting — 48

Precept 2: Primaries and caucuses — 50

Precept 3: Your vote is your voice — 52

Precept 4: You vote for a representative — 55

Precept 5: What if my candidate isn't elected? — 57

Proclaim: What does my vote mean? — 59

COMMANDMENT 5: HONOR THY FATHER AND THY MOTHER | 63

Principle: You and your candidates have to know the history and the laws surrounding government structure | 63

Precept 1 : The three types of government | 67

Precept 2: The Articles of Confederation through the end of Revolutionary War | 69

Precept 3: The Articles of Confederation after the Revolutionary War | 73

Precept 4: The Constitutional Convention | 75

Precept 5 : The three branches of government | 77

Precept 6: Checks and balances | 79

Precept 7: The United States: a democratic republic | 82

Precept 8: Congressional representation | 84

Precept 9: How the President is elected | 87

Precept 10: The Bill of Rights and other amendments | 89

Precept 11: Meaningful discussion | 92

Precept 12: Consistency and equality toward the law | 94

Proclaim: How do you feel about the Constitution, the government, and voting laws? | 97

COMMANDMENT 6: THOU SHALT NOT KILL | 101

Principle: Everyone has the right to life, liberty, and the pursuit of happiness | 101

Precept 1: Your candidates should recognize that all are created equal | 104

Precept 2: Your candidates should prioritize the rights of American citizens | 106

Precept 3: Your candidates should have clear plans for the interests of non-Americans | 108

Precept 4: Your candidates' views on crime and punishment | 110

Precept 5: Your candidates' stance on wars | 112

Proclaim: What does human life mean to you? | 115

TABLE OF CONTENTS

TABLE OF CONTENTS

COMMANDMENT 7: THOU SHALT NOT COMMIT ADULTERY — **119**

Principle: Families are the basic, fundamental, and most important unit of society — **119**

Precept 1 : Your candidates' family values — **122**

Precept 2: Your candidates' views on education — **124**

Precept 3: Your candidates' views on parental rights — **126**

Proclaim: What do families mean to you? — **129**

COMMANDMENT 8: THOU SHALT NOT STEAL — **133**

Principle: Economics — **133**

Precept 1: Your candidates should support the free market — **136**

Precept 2: Your candidates should treat America as the economic superpower — **139**

Precept 3: Your candidates should have a clear budget to handle economic issues — **141**

Precept 4: Taxes — **143**

Precept 5: Your candidates should support and help small businesses — **146**

Precept 6: Your candidates should encourage charitable giving — **149**

Procalim: How do you manage your economics? — **151**

TABLE OF CONTENTS

COMMANDMENT 9: THOU SHALT NOT BEAR FALSE WITNESS — **155**

Principle: Honesty — **155**

Precept 1 : Your candidates should avoid the three types of lies — **158**

Precept 2: Your candidates should respect the value of information — **161**

Precept 3: Your candidates should represent the level of honesty that you hope to display — **163**

Proclaim: Are you honest? — **165**

COMMANDMENT 10: THOU SHALT NOT COVET — **169**

Principle: Happiness — **169**

Precept 1: Happiness is infinite — **172**

Precept 2: Happiness comes from agency paired with righteousness — **174**

Precept 3: "Privilege" is a principle of oppression — **176**

Precept 4: Socialism is inherently covetous — **179**

Precept 5: Build your own happiness — **182**

Proclaim: How do you allow unfettered happiness? — **185**

CONCLUSION — **189**

Except the Lord build the house, they labour in vain that build it: except the Lord keep the city, the watchman waketh but in vain.

Psalm 127.

MomSquad

Introduction

Three months had passed since the Children of Israel were freed from bondage in Egypt. Moses was attempting to lead them to the promised land. They were fed manna in the wilderness, a constant reminder that they were being led and sustained by God. They knew they were God's chosen people, but they didn't know what that meant, what that looked like. They had been in bondage to the Egyptians for centuries, and had been somewhat cut off from God's teachings. What did God want for them? What were His rules? What did it look like to be God's people?

MomSquad

They arrived at a large mountain, called Sinai, and pitched their tents. Moses climbed to the top of Sinai to ask God what the Children of Israel should do, who they should be. The Lord gave this message for Moses to deliver to the Israelites:

"You yourselves have seen what I did to the Egyptians, and how I carried you on eagles' wings, and brought you to Myself. Now then, if you will indeed obey My voice and keep My covenant, then you shall be My own possession among all peoples, for all the earth is Mine; and you shall be to Me a kingdom of priests and a holy nation."

Genesis 19:4-6

When the Israelites heard these words they were ecstatic, and they cried:

"All that the Lord has spoken we will do."

Genesis 19:8

They were ready. Now they just needed to know how to do "all that the Lord has spoken."

The God of the Israelites would give them a strict code of 613 different commandments and regulations, called "The Law of Moses." 613 laws, however, can be extremely difficult to follow and understand. So, God gave Moses an overview. We know them as the **Ten Commandments**.

Written in God's own hand, they are considered the core of God's teachings. They highlight the most critical characteristics and behaviors that the Lord wanted the Children of Israel to have. They gave the minimum, the starting place, the foundation on which the Isralites could build. They were easy to understand and powerful to follow.

The purpose of this program is to help people center on eternal truth. The Ten Commandments is a great place to start. It doesn't matter if you are a devout practitioner of your faith, only go to church once or twice a year, don't know if you believe in God anymore, or are fully atheist. The Ten Commandments are a powerful guide.

With every election, we are bombarded with political ideas and opinions. One platform screams one thing; another screams something else.

All the while, social media explodes.

In the months leading to an election, Americans burn with political hysteria. Brother fights against brother, parents against children, friendships are lost. People are agitated and quick to anger

These things ought not to be.

But who do we vote for? What do we choose for our nation? How do we navigate such choppy waters? Where do we turn to know the truth?

Like the Israelites fresh from Egypt, we have dampened our connection to eternal truth. We crave that guidance and want our nation to be blessed. Still, it can be difficult to know where to start or how to even discern right from wrong.

This program is called:

The Ten Commandments and Voting

It will help you learn how to apply eternal truth to politics.

What you have in your hands is the Ten Commandments. Not ten rules for voting. Not ten recommendations for better political rhetoric. The Ten Commandments of the Old Testament. The Commandments that were given to the Israelites as the foundation. We are a nation blessed by God, and we should build upon eternal truth. This program will help you learn how to use the Ten Commandments as the core of your political beliefs. We are going to look at each commandment, understand what it means, and then apply those principles to voting and politics.

You will come to recognize the power of eternal truth. In your day-to-day life, in your long-term goals, in your religious practices, and in your families, truth and righteousness should be your guide. It should also guide your political, social, and patriotic duties.

In this book, each Commandment will have a core principle. That principle will guide you to make a "Proclamation." You will be proclaiming your beliefs, ideas, and feelings on each commandment, specifically focusing on how it relates to politics. You will also take time to compare your "Proclamation" with the political ideologies of your candidates. This will help you decide who you should vote for. We will not tell you how to vote. That is up to you. This is a tool to help you understand your own principles and politics, and decide who to vote for based on that understanding.

As you go through, each commandment will be broken up into Precepts. Each Precept will have a lesson where you will "Prepare" to answer questions. Each "Prepare" section will discuss how that Precept applies both to the Commandment and to voting. At the end of each Precept, there will be questions for you to "Ponder." These "Ponder" questions will help you get ready to make a "Proclamation."

As you move through the program, we hope you establish a stronger sense of personal values, as well as learn some of the history and content of the Constitution. Use this as an opportunity to learn about yourself and what you hope to see in your candidates. Learn to apply eternal truth to every aspect of your life

MomSquad

This book **will** help you vote.

You **will** be guided you through a study of American voting so that you can pick the best candidate.

You **will** learn how to find your core values and principles as you center yourself on eternal truth.

You **will** look at your candidates, and the voting process, and measure your candidates against your personal values.

You **will** focus on the idea of eternal truth, using the Biblical Ten Commandments.

You **will NOT** be told who to vote for. Instead you will develop your personal values so that you can choose for yourself.

MomSquad

How to Use this Program

This segment, "How to Use this Program" will guide you through the basic format of *The Ten Commandments and Voting*, so that you are ready to center on **eternal truth**, and make wise election choices.

The program is divided into ten sections called **Commandments.**

Each Commandment, taken directly from Exodus, is the starting point to guide your study of voting in the United States.

Commandments will address one overarching **Principle** that will help you to apply the Commandments to voting in the United States.

To help you understand each Principle, the Commandments will be broken down into smaller **Precepts**.

Each Principle and its Precepts will give guidance to help you center on eternal truth and develop personal values, but they will not tell you what, specifically, to think.

Your views are up to you.

This program is meant to increase your toolbox so that you can develop on your own.

Navigation

This workbook is organized according to the following general formula:

Example

Commandment

Ethical framework of human responsibilities found in the Old Testament.

Principle

Foundational truth, proposition, belief, or behavior that will be the focus for each Commandment.

Precept

Nuanced topics of study that will allow you to dig through and understand the Principle and Commandment more clearly.

Prepare

These sections will hold the main body of the program and are where you will do the bulk of your study. They will flesh out the Commandments, Principles, and Precepts.

MomSquad

Ponder

A question to help you think about the Precept you just learned. This is a moment for you to reflect and apply the teachings to yourself. Feel free to write paragraphs upon paragraphs, or just a few words. You can even skip these if you really want, (though it's in your best interest to write something).

Proclaim

These are the most important parts of this program. This is where you Proclaim your answer to a grand question pertaining to the Commandment. You will write both your own proclamation and what you think the candidates will answer. Then you will and compare and contrast. The Proclaim sections are where the teachings become actionable. You can look at the candidates and choose based on your values.

Use this book as a tool to help you as you decide who to vote for and choose what eternal truths you want to center your life upon.

Godspeed.

MomSquad

Momsquad

MomSquad.com

Commandment 1

"Thou shalt have no other gods before Me"

Principle

Center on eternal truth

Precepts

1. Both you and your candidates should have a clear moral center based on eternal truth
2. Some "gods" are not based on eternal truth
3. Governments exist to secure "the Laws of Nature and of Nature's God." In other words, governments should codify eternal truth into a societal structure

MomSquad

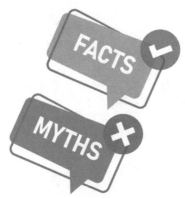

Prepare

How can I discern the central truths I build my life around?

Commandment 1 tells us to put God first. When we center on eternal truth, everything else in our life falls into place. God gave this Commandment to Moses because He did not want His people to give their hearts, souls, and minds to the wrong thing. He wanted his people to center their lives on Him. If we put God first, our lives and our nation will have the greatest potential for true happiness.

"God," especially in the Judeo-Christian sense, is an eternal, omniscient being that commands and guides the universe. God is all-knowing, all-powerful, omnipresent, and benevolent. For many, such a grand being can feel distant. Others may not even believe that such a being exists. Yet we are asked to put this "God" first, to "have no other gods before him."

So how do we do it? How do we put "God" first? We seek eternal truth. We find ways to center ourselves: morals, values, and beliefs that are always true. Even if you don't believe in God (with a capital "G") you can find the eternal truths that light your soul and guide your life.

For the rest of this program, the words "god(s)" and "eternal truth" will be used interchangeably. When we refer to "God" the being, it will have a capital "G."

For voting, Commandment 1 will take you through three Precepts:

1. Both you and your candidates should have a clear moral center based on eternal truth.
2. Man can create gods that are not based on eternal truth.
3. Governments exist to secure "the Laws of Nature and of Nature's God." In other words, governments should codify eternal truth into a societal structure.

By the end of your study of Commandment 1, you will be able to Proclaim, "Who and what are your gods?" That is to say. "What eternal truths do you center on?" Even if you believe in God and put Him first, we still encourage you to examine yourself, and look at the eternal truths that you center your life on. We also encourage you to ask it of the candidates you are considering voting for, and honestly examine what their answers may be.

Who/what are your gods?

*In all cases to follow **truth** as the only safe guide.*

Thomas Jefferson

You and your candidates should have a clear moral center based on eternal truth

Prepare

To have a clear moral center based on eternal truth, we have to know what truth is.

Truth is knowledge and understanding. It cannot be created and has no end. It is clear. It is simple. It builds upon itself. It leads to goodness. It does not try to trick, confuse, or hide. Truth is always true. 1+1 will always equal 2. It helps us to discern good from evil. It is the antithesis of deception. It sets us free.

Put simply, truth is an understanding of the past, the present, and the future.

We can know the past by studying history, writings, teachings, and the great literature of the world; we know the past by educating ourselves of the human legacy. We can know the present by our own experience, our own personal understanding of the world, our values, our principles, our beliefs, our passions, and our education; who we are helps us to understand the present. We can understand the future by a combination of the past and the present; we apply our understanding of the past with our experience of the present, and we can prepare for the future.

4

Truth   Lies

happiness. Eternal truth is typically focused outward, pushing people to serve others' needs over their own.

Find what your gods are. What do you worship with your heart, might, mind, and soul? What do your pursuits, actions, thoughts, etc. say about your core values? Make changes if necessary.

Eternal truth is truth that builds humankind. It heals the heart and is an anchor for the soul. "I am valuable and worthy of love, and forgiveness" is an eternal truth. "All men are created equal" is an eternal truth. Find what builds you, heals your heart, anchors your soul, and helps you to understand the past, present, and future.

Eternal truth should guide your life, your candidate, and the nation.

To "put god first" is to center on eternal truth, to center your morals, your personal values, your beliefs, and your actions. As you find truth, hold fast to it.

Center yourself on something you trust. It could be God Himself. It could be family. It could be clarity and simplicity. It could be true lasting

Find what your candidates' gods are. What do they worship with their heart, might, mind, and soul. What do their pursuits, actions, thoughts, etc. say about their core values?

Personal values should be extremely clear to you. They should not simply be a concept that is vaguely understood. Both in your own life and for your candidates, values should be articulable, actionable, and conspicuous.

While values should always be rooted in eternal truth, what you value will change over the course of your life. A five-year-old is different from a high schooler and different from a parent. That shift is not a bad thing, but it is something to be aware of. If your candidates' values have changed over time, evaluate why. How have they changed? Do you like the changes? Are the chnages centered on eternal truth?

COMMANDMENT 1

Ponder

Ponder

What are your personal values?

Ponder

Ponder

What truth(s) do you center on?

If you have more to say, additional space is available at the back of the book.

Man can create gods that are not based on eternal truths

Prepare

Similar to eternal truths, man-made gods are grand ideas. They are the overarching forces that can, and often do, drive people away from eternal truth. They are concepts. They are beliefs, motives, and ideas that simply exist. They are propagated by man, usually for personal gain.

Greed. Popularity. Power. Wealth. Influence. Prominence. Prestige. Fear. Violence. War. Appearance. Pride. Gluttony. Sloth. Lust. Science. Expertise. Status. Envy. Etc.

These are not always bad, in and of themselves. Wealth and influence, for example, are often used to enact great good in the world. The issue is when these gods receive our worship; when people choose to center on these, often self-serving principles, rather than eternal truth; when these come before God.

Your gods will be the ultimate authority in your life. Eternal truth leads people to look outwardly. Man-made gods lead people to serve their own interests. Those who follow man-made gods are led to a sense of privilege and entitlement that stems from a lack of self-worth. They look for easy success, often to the detriment of those around them. Man-made gods pull people away from goodness, toward a fleeting high, toward a false sense of happiness.

7

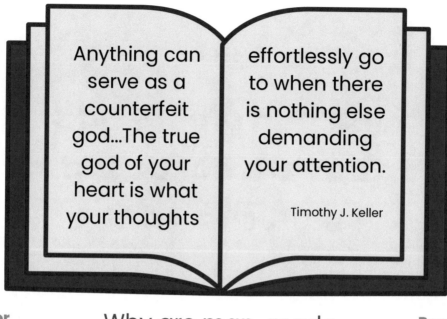

Anything can serve as a counterfeit god...The true god of your heart is what your thoughts effortlessly go to when there is nothing else demanding your attention.

Timothy J. Keller

Ponder

Why are man-made gods so dangerous?

Ponder

Ponder

How can we tell the difference between man-made gods and eternal truth?

Ponder

If you have more to say, additional space is available at the back of the book.

Governments exist to secure "The Laws of Nature and of Nature's God" In other words, governments should codify eternal truth into a societal structure

Prepare

This program is called, "The Ten Commandments and Voting." Up to this point, we have discussed eternal truth as it pertains to you. This precept will focus on truth's relation to voting and government.

The most famous line in the Declaration of Independence is, "We hold these truths to be self-evident, that all men are created equal, that they are endowed by their Creator with certain unalienable Rights, that among these are Life, Liberty and the pursuit of Happiness." Essentially, God gives all people the right to life, liberty, and the pursuit of happiness.

The next sentence in the Declaration of Independence is equally important. "That to secure these rights, Governments are instituted among Men, deriving their just powers from the consent of the governed." Jefferson wanted this to be crystal clear. The purpose of government is to secure life, liberty, and the pursuit of happiness. Governments are made to protect your rights, and they get their power directly from you.

Continuing in the Declaration of Independence:

It is the Right of the People...to institute [a] Government, laying its foundation on such principles and organizing its power in such form, as to them shall seem most likely to effect their Safety and Happiness.

The foundation of the government should be principles of happiness. It should be eternal truth. The government should "organize its power" to reflect that truth. Government should consist of eternal truths put into a societal structure.

Ponder

What truth do you want secured by our government?

Ponder

If you have more to say, additional space is available at the back of the book.

C O M M A N D M E N T 1

Proclaim your beliefs about Commandment 1 and voting

Look back at what you have written as you studied Commandment 1

As you studied, you may have written paragraphs upon paragraphs, a few words, or nothing at all. Whatever you wrote is completely fine. However, right now, you are invited to truly take a moment and proclaim in writing:

Who and/or what are your gods?

Put as much or as little as you like, but put something. Put something that you can say honestly, shamelessly even. It may even be aspirational. That's great! There may be something that you write down that you feel you need to change.

That's great too! This is a time to reflect as well as proclaim. Let this be something that guides you.

Then take a few more minutes to ponder any upcoming elections. With the candidates involved, who and/or what are their gods?

Take an honest look. Don't just put down what you want to be true because your emotions about it are heightened or because they are a member of your political party. Truly and honestly, who and/or what are the candidates' gods?

Who and/or what are my gods?

**C
O
M
M
A
N
D
M
E
N
T

1**

If you have more to say, additional space is available at the back of the book.

Who and/or what are my candidates' gods?

COMMANDMENT 1

If you have more to say, additional space is available at the back of the book.

Now compare.
How do the candidates match up with your own personal views?
Where are they the same? Where are they different?

COMMANDMENT 1

My gods

My candidates' gods

Same

Same

Different

Different

If you have more to say, additional space is available at the back of the book.

TOP. ODD

Commandment 2

"Thou shalt not make unto thee any graven image"

Principle

Graven images are the tangible manifestations of your gods

Precepts

1. Political parties can be graven images
2. Policies and hot-button issues can be graven images

MomSquad

How can I discern the manifestations of my gods?

COMMANDMENT 2

This Commandment is closely intertwined with Commandment 1. Our gods will lead us to imagery, that is, manifestations of our gods in the world. "Graven images" in this course, will refer to the tangible manifestations and representations of our gods. They are tools to help us in worshiping and following our gods. When they come from eternal truth, they can increase our lasting happiness. When they come from man-made gods, they can be devastating, as they are the tangible manifestations of the ideas and powers that compose those man-made gods. You will dig into the purpose and dangers of graven images later on in your study of this Commandment.

God (with a capital "G") is a God of imagery. He teaches people using images, signs, tokens, stories, etc. He regularly gives imagery for His people to use in worship and religious practice. For example, the Arc of the Covenant, prophets, scriptures, the sacrament, etc. These images and expressions of God can help us to look toward Him and understand His plan.

The issue is not in the images themselves. Graven images are not inherently bad because eternal truth will always have images, that is, tangible manifestations in the world. The issue is in making "unto thee" a graven image, making your own manifestation of a man-made god. Man-made gods need man-made images. Those man-made images pull people away from eternal truth, if we are not properly centered.

A man-made god "popularity" might have the graven image of social media. Another man-made god "appearance" might have the graven images of a weight room, steroids, makeup, eating disorders, or high fashion.

Much like the gods they are made for, man's graven images are not inherently bad. Social media can be a huge force for good. A weight room or makeup can be excellent tools to improve one's life. However, they can also become consumptive, ruining self-image, pushing for more intense habits and practices, and causing potentially irreparable damage.

The physical manifestations of our gods should point us back to eternal truth. (A wedding band, pointing us to our spouse. A book of scripture pointing us back to God.) That's not to say that we can't benefit from man-made images. The gold that was used for the golden calf in Exodus was still valuable as gold. We just need to make sure that we are not bowing to the images. The things we do should point us back to eternal truth. God should come first. Truth should come first. How we are centered will guide our use of graven images.

For voting, Commandment 2 will take you through 2 Precepts:

1. Political parties can be graven images.
2. Policies and hot-button issues can be graven images.

By the end of your study of Commandment 2, you will be able to Proclaim, "What are the manifestations of your gods?" We encourage you to focus on this as you study for yourself, as well as ask it of the candidates you are considering voting for.

What are the manifestations of your gods?

"Man's nature, so to speak, is a perpetual factory of idols."

John Calvin

17

Political parties can be graven images

Prepare

Political parties are powerful tools for politics and elections. However, they can also be a graven image of power and influence. Too often people bow to their political parties. They value party loyalty over their own values and ideals.

Still, we have to navigate political parties. Our government operates around a two-party system. For hundreds of years, there have been two prevailing political parties. What those parties were, and what they stood for, have shifted. However, the presence of these parties has defined American politics.

Parties are excellent tools to help like-minded people come together. It allows people to enact change, enforce policies, remove policies, etc. It also helps to unify large groups on political issues, summarize the general trends of a politician, and elect candidates. They can be incredibly powerful forces for good, and are an integral part of the political climate.

lead to divisiveness, fanaticism, and demonizing of opposing viewpoints. In his farewell address, Washington warned of the dangers of political parties.

Because they have been around for so long, much of the political process is based on a partied system, especially a two party system. Voting polls and primaries integrate parties; congressional representation is discussed in terms of the party system; voting policies for the people's approval of new laws is based on the party system; policies and individuals are discussed as right-leaning or left-leaning, which automatically aligns them with an already established political party; the list goes on.

Parties are integral parts of the political system because it is in our nature to develop groups and communities. Like-minded people have always gathered. It allows them to find strength and enact greater change.

Be wary, though, of political parties. Much like a sports team, parties can

"They serve to organize faction, to give it an artificial and extraordinary force—to put in the place of the delegated will of the nation, the will of a party; often a small but artful and enterprising minority of the community… However combinations or associations of the above description may, now and then, answer popular ends, they are likely, in the course of time and things, to become potent engines by which cunning, ambitious, and unprincipled men will be enabled to subvert the power of the people and to usurp for themselves the reins of government, destroying afterwards the very engines which have lifted them to unjust dominion."

In other words, while political parties are useful, they are easy to take advantage of. Strong rhetoric and party loyalty allow a powerful minority to use political parties for personal gain. Individuals and small groups are able to bend the will of the nation by bending the will of an individual party. The party becomes a graven image that can be leveraged to pull people away from eternal truth.

The power of the people lies in each person's personal values. The degree to which people know and live their values determines the success of the nation. Your loyalties are to God and eternal truth first, your family second, and your nation third. Political parties come later. Your loyalties lie in what you value. You are not defined by your political party. You are far more than a cry for red or blue. You are a child of God. Do not make a graven image of your political party. Do not put your party over your values. The fanaticism, division, and dangers that attend political parties, (the extremely violent protests in the name of social justice, the run on the Capitol, the anti-semitic chants on college campuses) occur when people put loyalty to their party over loyalty to their values. Political parties should be a tool to help you promote your values, not a group that defines them for you.

Ponder

Have I made a graven image of my party?

Ponder

If you have more to say, additional space is available at the back of the book.

Policies and hot-button issues can be graven images

Prepare

Policies are the manifestations of your god in the political and legal sphere. Policies, like government, should be built on eternal truth. They should reflect the fact that we have put eternal truth before our own desires. Sadly, that does not always happen.

When you examine political policies, you can see what truths they are built upon. You can see what god they serve. Often, people use hot-button issues to create a sense of fanaticism and panic. They capitalize on the mania of these hot-button issues to confuse people and lead them away from eternal truth.

That is why hot-button issues are so divisive. They pull us in every direction. Candidates will often use them to confuse, distract, or entice voters. The hot-button issues become graven images.

Don't worship policies. Center yourself on truth, and then measure policies and issues against that truth. When you evaluate government practices, they should be seen through the lens of your values. This becomes increasingly easy as you come to know who you are and what you value. It also means that it is your responsibility to learn government policies. When a new bill is passed, you should study it. When elections happen, research the candidates. When major events occur, get informed from trustworthy sources. Understand how those all measure up against your personal values.

Stephen R. Covey

Happiness, like unhappiness, is a proactive choice.

Ponder

Ponder

What policies do you support and what truths are they built upon?

If you have more to say, additional space is available at the back of the book.

Proclaim your beliefs about Commandment 2 and voting

Look back at what you have written as you studied Commandment 2

As you studied, you may have written paragraphs upon paragraphs, a few words, or nothing at all. Whatever you wrote is completely fine. However, right now, we invite you to truly take a moment and proclaim in writing:

What are the manifestations of your gods?

Put as much or as little as you like, but put something. Put something that you can say honestly, shamelessly even. It may even be aspirational. That's great! There may be something that you write down that you feel you need to change. That's great too! This is a time to reflect as well as proclaim. Let this be something that guides you.

Then take a few more minutes to ponder any upcoming elections. With the candidates involved, what are the manifestations of their gods?

Take an honest look. Don't just put down what you want to be true because your emotions about it are heightened or because they are from your political party. Truly and honestly, what are the manifestations of your candidates' gods?

23

What are the manifestations of my gods?

COMMANDMENT 2

24

If you have more to say, additional space is available at the back of the book.

What are the manifestations of my candidates' gods?

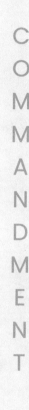

COMMANDMENT 2

25

If you have more to say, additional space is available at the back of the book.

Now compare.
How do the candidates match up with your own personal views?
Where are they the same? Where are they different?

COMMANDMENT 2

My manifestations

Same

Different

My candidates' manifestations

Same

Different

If you have more to say, additional space is available at the back of the book.

Commandment 3

"Thou shalt not take the name of the Lord thy God in vain"

Principle

The Name of God is I Am

Precepts

1. How someone speaks of themself reflects their gods
2. How someone speaks of others reflects their gods
3. The names of graven images reflect who/what your gods are
4. How you and your candidates treat others in political discourse reflects your gods

27

Prepare

What do the names that I use say about me, others, and my gods?

In the bible, God calls himself the Great I Am. "I Am that I Am" He says (Exodus 3). We speak of ourselves, of others, even things by a name or title. "My father," "a chair," "my name is..." The way we speak illustrates how we think, what we believe, and how we will act.

In the Bible, James tells us:

For in many things we offend all. If any man offend not in word, the same is a perfect man, and able also to bridle the whole body.

James 3:2

Names are not a light thing. Words are not a light thing. The Hebrew God gave Adam dominion over the earth and told him to name the animals. In so doing, He made Adam responsible for the creatures AND the words to describe them. The words we use to describe ourselves and others have great power.

In fact, when we hear our own name, our brains have the same response we have when we participate in actions that align with our core identities. Strip a person of their name and you separate them from their sense of self and community connection. The names and words we use define us. They should be treated with the

28

utmost reverence. God's children deserve dignity and respect simply because they are the children of God.

Name calling, insults, profanities, etc. will almost never stem from eternal truth. Remember, eternal truth looks outward, and seeks to build others. There is real power in language. There is real power in words. Speak with conviction. Speak truth.

In the political sphere, we must treat our rights with respect. We must treat others with respect. Politics is the tool through which we can codify and protect eternal truth. Treat it as such. Politics and political discussion are meant to build up this nation and make it better, not tear it down and divide it. Do not degrade and demonize others in political discussion.

For voting, Commandment 3 will take you through four Precepts:

1. How someone speaks of themself reflects their gods.
2. How someone speaks of others reflects their gods.
3. The names of graven images reflect who/what your gods are.
4. How you and your candidates treat others in political discourse reflects your gods.

By the end of your study of Commandment 3, you will be able to Proclaim, "What are the names associated with your god/gods?" We encourage you to focus on this as you study for yourself, as well as ask it of the candidates you are considering voting for.

What are the names associated with your god/gods?

What is in a name?

William Shakespeare

How someone speaks of themself reflects their gods

Prepare

God is the great I Am. We are His children. Eternal truth is eternal. We are built upon that unchanging truth. When we follow eternal truth, when we recognize ourselves as children of God, we speak differently of ourselves.

When our candidates are centered on eternal truth, they speak differently of themselves.

How do you speak of yourself? Do you speak as a follower of God, as someone centered on great eternal truth?

Those who follow God, who speak and act as His children, act and serve in His name. When we are centered on eternal truth we speak with confidence and conviction, not arrogance. Are you confident? Are you insecure? Are you arrogant? What about your candidate? Are they confident? Arrogant? Insecure?

Labels hold meaning. When we are sitting in a chair, we call it, "chair." We might even say, "office chair" or "cushy chair." These labels help us to

yourself sad, you are more likely to be sad. If you say you are superior and more valuable than others, you will treat others as lesser. Some of you might be even thinking, "I can't believe it. I think badly of myself all the time. I'm hurting myself for it! I'm so stupid! Why do I keep doing that?" That kind of thinking is exactly what we're talking about. Take a deep breath. Applaud yourself for being aware, and then move forward.

know what the item is, what it's used for, and how it's beneficial. If you were to say, "the ugly chair" or "the bad chair" or "the broken chair," your opinion toward that chair would change, negatively. The words and labels used to describe the chair hold weight over your view of the chair.

The words you use to describe yourself hold weight over who you are. We often use inaccurate or incorrect names to hide our true character. We especially hide our own goodness because we are afraid of our full potential. When you assign yourself names that are unduly self abasing or self aggrandizing, you change your view of yourself. You change who you are. If you call yourself lazy, you are more likely to be lazy. If you call

It is trendy to assign as many labels as possible to yourself. Do not buy into that trend. Most labels are divisive and inaccurate. They put people in boxes and groups rather than addressing that each person is their own individual. People in positions of power often use these group-labels so that they can throw out blanket "solutions." They leverage these "solutions" for their own political or social gain. When you

By centering our lives on eternal truth, we know who we are. Humanity is the pinnacle of the creations of the universe. You carry that blessing, that responsibility. You must speak and act accordingly. Speak truthfully of yourself.

center on eternal truth, knowing what you need becomes easier. We must seek truth in all things, even in the thoughts and names we give to ourselves.

Those who follow man and man-made gods often speak and act as if they serve themselves. They act in their own selfish interests. They act in their own glory. Man-made gods glorify man. Eternal truth glorifies truth.

Ponder

What do I say of myself?

Ponder

If you have more to say, additional space is available at the back of the book.

How someone speaks of others reflects their gods

Prepare

As human beings, children of the great I Am, we are equal. We hold that truth "to be self-evident, that all men are created equal." Those around us should be treated with dignity and respect simply because they, too, are purveyors of eternal truth.

You have a set of personal values. Those personal values are important to you; they help you understand who you are. Your candidate has a set of personal values. Other people have personal values. Those personal values are important to them and help them

understand who they are. Often, your values will not align with someone else's values. That is okay. Even if you disagree with a candidate on every issue, that's okay.

In fact, that's the point. If everyone was going to have the same set of values with the same life focus and the same goals, what would be the purpose of individual liberties? We could simply make a system that forces everyone to live in a regimented and perfected "utopia" where no one is different from anyone else. Freedoms and rights would become obsolete if everyone was the same. But we are not the same. That's the beauty. We're unique and beautiful. We have been given the chance to grow and change and find out what's important to us, to become something greater than we are now. Everyone deserves that chance.

Now. Does that mean that you are passive? No. Does that mean that your candidate should simply bow to the whims of someone else's beliefs? No. You should stand up for what you believe. Your candidates should definitely stand firm in their beliefs. You can debate. You can argue. But you cannot take away someone else's right to think and believe.

Your stewardship is over yourself. You get to determine who you are. No one else has the right to decide that for you. Conversely, you do not have the right

to decide who someone else is. They are their own stewards. These God-given rights merit our respect, and the choices people make when exercising those rights also merit our respect. Ours is not to choose how others live. Ours is to choose for ourselves.

You will meet opposing viewpoints. Those people have a God-given right to believe what they believe. You are powerless to deny them that right. Your candidates are powerless to deny them that right. You can debate and discuss, but canceling someone, shutting someone down, belittling someone, exercising your will over someone else because of their personal values or views is contrary to the nature of eternal truth.

Do not take God's name in vain. He has given both to you and to them. Hold the right to disagree in high regard, and ask that they do the same.

> There seems to be a lot of name calling going on, but I want to remind you of what our good old dad told me one time. Labels are for soup cans.

George W. Bush

The way you speak of others reflects the way you see them. The way your candidate speaks of others reflects the way they see others. Are other people seen as children of God, purveyors of eternal truth? Or are they "less than?" Are they someone or something that is in your way? Are they a stepping stone? Are they stupid? Uninformed? Brainwashed? Does your candidate mostly glorify themselves when they speak of others? That is a sign of the gods they serve. Do they build and edify when they speak of others? That is also a sign of the gods they serve.

Ponder

What do I say of others?

Ponder

If you have more to say, additional space is available at the back of the book.

The names of graven images reflect who/what your gods are

Prepare

As we've said before, graven images are the manifestations of your god or gods. You have examined your graven images. Now look at what you call them? What are they to you? What about your candidates? What do they say of their party? Of the opposing party? Of their policies?

What about addictions? Hidden activities? Do you or your candidates have those? What do you call them?

Do you have things that bring you true joy? Do you have accomplishments and memories that remind you of who you are and what you are capable of? What do you call these things? What do you say of them? How do you identify your graven images to yourself and others? How do you paint them in your life?

Look at where you spend your time, effort and energy. Look at what it points to. Do the same for your candidate.

Look at the language and words used to talk about activities, actions, policies, etc. What does that say about those things? What does that say about who your gods are? What does that say about your candidate's gods?

Names are deeply embedded, and when we say them, we call forth the spirit of the thing. We now know this from science. The mind does not distinguish between the real thing and the imagined thing. To a thirsty person, both real water and imagined water increase their thirst. The line between the names and the things themselves is not so clear as we might believe. And so by our speaking a thing's name, we call it into existence.

Ewan Townhead

Ponder

Ponder

What do I and my candidates say of our graven images?

If you have more to say, additional space is available at the back of the book.

How you and your candidates treat others in political discourse reflects your gods

Prepare

We already discussed that the way we speak of others reflects our gods, but, because this is about voting, we should discuss political discourse.

The way people speak of others in the political sphere reflects the truths that guide their political thoughts. Political opinions should be guided by personal values and centered on eternal truth. When the framers wrote the Constitution, they protected our God-given rights. They created a system of checks and balances to ensure that the federal government could not get too powerful. They also instituted protections to individual rights, known as the Bill of Rights. The Constitution and its amendments are meant to help individuals enjoy the liberties and protections given to them by God.

As citizens our job is to not only enjoy those rights, but to protect them for other people. No matter who they are, citizens of the United States are promised rights and protections based solely on the fact that they are a citizen. That is part of America's majesty. The darkest parts of American history stem from people losing sight of that equality. Everyone is equally protected by the Constitution, a fact that should be both celebrated and safeguarded, especially by politicians.

Everyone is unique. That is what makes these Constitutional protections so fantastic. As children of God, everyone can exercise their rights as they see fit. Generally speaking, as long as actions do not infringe on the rights and properties of others, those actions are protected.

Do what you want with your rights. Make your life what you want it to be. As mentioned before, this is not encouraging a passive stance when it comes to government issues. The point of voting, democracy, and representative government is to help promote and codify eternal truth through law and governance. In a republic, debate is essential. Democratic systems require dissenting opinions. That kind of discussion is how we arrived at the Constitution in the first place.

You and your candidates should be active advocates. If, for example, you want education reforms, say so. If a candidate wants a law passed or repealed, they should say so. Be ready and willing to engage in debates and discussions about important political issues.

People should feel edified and uplifted from political debates. If both sides honestly discuss the merits and weaknesses of policies, propositions, candidates, etc., political discussion will not become adversarial. Your candidate should make informed claims and genuinely listen to others instead of tearing them down. You should do the same. This is especially important when the person you are speaking to does not offer you the same courtesy. Be better. Hold yourself to the higher standard of eternal truth. Build people up.

Let's put this in the clearest possible terms. This standard applies to you and your candidate. Don't be mean in political discourse. Don't call people names. Don't use profanity. Don't drop aggressive buzz words and labels like racist, bigot, socialist, leftist, alt-right, nazi, antisemitic, terrorist, anti-American, un-American, etc. Name calling and aggressive labeling destroy productive discussion. Don't lump whole groups of people into one single-minded body, such as millennials, college students, the left, the right, socialists, racial groups, women, men, lgbtq+, boomers, mothers, religious groups, etc. These types of hasty generalizations rarely hold water in informed political discourse, and stifle the nuance that should attend political discussion. Above all, don't assume what the other person's argument is. Rather, listen to and understand what that person thinks, what they value, and why they value it. Ask questions. Seek understanding, even and especially if you disagree with the person. Chances are they have legitimate reasons to think and believe those things. You do not have to agree, but try to understand different viewpoints. Understanding other viewpoints will enable legitimate and productive discourse.

Martin Luther King jr.

"You have very little morally persuasive power with people who can feel your underlying contempt."

Ponder

Ponder

How do I speak of and treat others who have different political ideals than me?

If you have more to say, additional space is available at the back of the book.

Proclaim your beliefs about Commandment 3 and voting

Look back at what you have written as you studied Commandment 3

As you studied, you may have written paragraphs upon paragraphs, a few words, or nothing at all. Whatever you wrote is completely fine. However, right now, we invite you to truly take a moment and proclaim in writing:

What are the names associated with your gods?

Put as much or as little as you like, but put something. Put something that you can say honestly, shamelessly even. It may even be aspirational. That's great! There may be something that you write down that you feel you need to change. That's great too! This is a time to reflect as well as proclaim. Let this be something that guides you.

Then take a few more minutes to ponder any upcoming elections. With the candidates involved, what are the names associated with their gods?

Take an honest look. Don't just put down what you want to be true because your emotions about it are heightened or because they are from your political party. Truly and honestly, what are the names of your candidates' gods?

What are the names associated with my gods?

COMMANDMENT 3

If you have more to say, additional space is available at the back of the book.

What are the names associated with my candidates' gods?

43

If you have more to say, additional space is available at the back of the book.

Now compare.
How do the candidates match up with your own personal views?
Where are they the same? Where are they different?

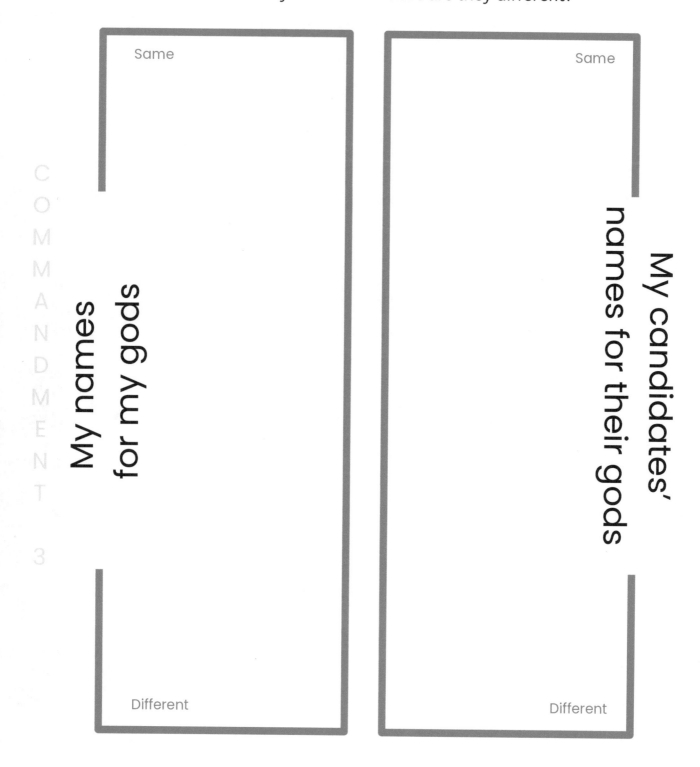

COMMANDMENT 3

Same

My names
for my gods

Different

Same

My candidates'
names for their gods

Different

If you have more to say, additional space is available at the back of the book.

Commandment 4

"Remember the Sabbath Day to Keep it Holy"

Principle

There is a time set apart to vote, and voting is a sacred responsibility

Precepts

1. The process of voting
2. Primaries and caucuses
3. Your vote is your voice
4. You vote for a representative
5. What if my candidate isn't elected?

MomSquad

Prepare

How can I prepare for the sacred responsibility of voting?

COMMANDMENT

4

The fourth commandment that God gave to Moses was to set aside one day per week for worship. That day is called the Sabbath. We need to prioritize time to center ourselves on eternal truth. Our time is scared. Goodness will not happen by accident. Eternal truth is usually found by those who seek it. So seek. This doesn't have to be a quiet mediation or hard focused study. You can seek eternal truth by participating in inspired institutions.

Our government is an institution that was built upon the foundation of eternal truth. It codifies eternal truth by protecting rights. Our government is a government of the people, by the people, and for the people. Because of that, our direct participation is meaningful. It is a chance to seek eternal truth. One of the most sacred opportunities that we have is the right to vote. We must give that right its due import, and make time to study and learn. On voting day, we should put aside other things and focus on voting. Take an active role in that inspired institution. Voting is a sacred responsibility that we all must take seriously.

Voting is a civic sacrament.

Rev. Theodore Hesburgh

For voting, Commandment 4 will take you through five precepts:

1. The process of voting.
2. Primaries and caucuses.
3. Your vote is your voice.
4. You vote for a representative
5. What if my candidate isn't elected.

By the end of your study of Commandment 4, you will be able to Proclaim, "What does my vote mean?" We encourage you to focus on this as you study for yourself, as well as ask it of the candidates you are considering voting for.

What does my vote mean?

Article 1 of the Constitution made states responsible for overseeing federal elections. Since then we have made four amendments regarding voting in America.

- **15th Amendment**: African American men got the right to vote in 1870, but some states still imposed barriers.

- The **19th Amendment**: Women finally got the right to vote in 1920.

- The **24th Amendment**: Poll taxes, literacy tests and other blocks that some states used to keep African Americans from voting were banned in 1964.

- The **26th Amendment**: Ratified in 1971, this amendment lowered the voting age for all elections to 18.

The process of voting

Prepare

Voting is a process. To a certain degree it is extremely simple. You put down what candidate you are voting for, your vote is cast, and then you wait for the results. If that's what your voting experience has been, that's great! You have participated in one of the great blessings of the  American government. There is, however, far more to voting. Voting eligibility is relatively simple. You have to be a legal adult citizen and a resident of the precinct you're voting in.

Let's break that down. You have to be 18 or older to vote. For some states that age requirement is requisite in both primary and general elections. In other states, you can vote in primary elections at age 17, if you turn 18 on or before the general election. You also have to be a citizen of the United States and live in the state/municipality in which you vote. You vote to elect your representatives, so you must live where you are going to be represented.

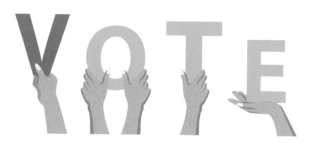

North Dakota does not even require voters to register. When you register to vote, you accomplish two major tasks. You prepare yourself to vote when an election occurs, and you officially register as part of a political party. Registering as a part of a party does not have much effect in the general election. However, it holds significant sway during primary elections.

You also have to register to vote. How you register will vary from state to state. In many states you can register to vote when you receive a driver's license. In most states you can also register to vote online. Interestingly,

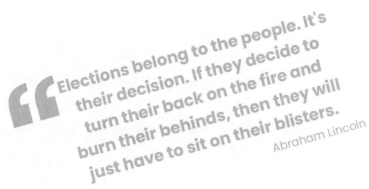

"Elections belong to the people. It's their decision. If they decide to turn their back on the fire and burn their behinds, then they will just have to sit on their blisters.

Abraham Lincoln

Ponder

How does my city/state manage elections?

Ponder

49

If you have more to say, additional space is available at the back of the book.

Primaries and caucuses

Prepare

Primary elections are often used as a catch-all term for primaries and caucuses. Generally, in an election, there are two sets of campaigns. The first is a campaign to win the nomination within a political party. The second is a campaign to win the actual election and be elected to office. The first election typically occurs within a political party, so that that party can nominate the candidate that they support most. This occurs in two ways, through a primary or through a caucus.

A primary is run by a state or local government. It is, typically, an election in which only voters who are registered with a particular political party can vote for the candidate of that party. Whoever wins is the nominee.

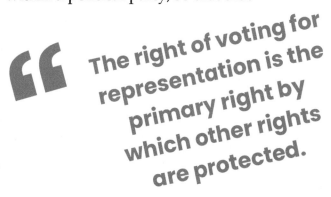

" The right of voting for representation is the primary right by which other rights are protected.

Thomas Paine

50

delegate votes on behalf of the caucus in the next round. The process of electing a delegate is usually done by direct vote or by forming groups of committed and uncommitted voters. Caucuses often occur at conventions where candidates or representatives of those candidates can give speeches, presentations, and arguments to persuade voters.

A caucus is run by a political party rather than a government. It is a meeting in which members of that political party will discuss, debate, and eventually vote on a candidate. How that discussion and voting occurs will vary from one caucus to the next. Generally speaking, there will be multiple rounds of caucus voting. First the caucus elects a delegate. Then that

So to clarify, primaries are run by a state or local government, with private votes, and are a lot like a small version of a general election. Caucuses are run by political parties, have private or public votes, and are a lot like town hall meetings, with speeches, debates, and persuasive arguments.

Ponder　　　　Will I participate in a primary or a caucus? What do those look like where I live?　　　　**Ponder**

If you have more to say, additional space is available at the back of the book.

Your vote is your voice

C
O
M
M
A
N
D
M
E
N
T

4

Prepare

America is a democratic republic. We are a representative government, with a democratic vote (more on that in Commandment 5). When you vote, you get to have a say in a government that would otherwise be governed without your input. Your voice, your opinion, your influence matters to government officials because you have a vote.

Voting is a patriotic duty that we should take seriously. It should never be a mere cry for red or blue. That's not to say that you can't vote for one of the two major political parties. As mentioned before, those parties can be great forces for positive change. However, your vote should not simply be cast out of party

devotion or even out of a desire to win an election. Even more so, you should never consider that your vote is meaningless.

Your vote is your voice, so vote to be heard.

We are a republic, with literally hundreds of representatives in government. Those representatives hold significant sway over the government, and your life. Interestingly, the president is the poorest at representing the voice of the people because they are just one person.

The closer an elected official is to you, the more they will influence your life. Your mayor has more influence in your life than your governor who has more influence than your president. If you want to see real change and in your life and community, start at the local level. True change happens locally first, then the state and federal levels.

It's a beautiful day in the neighborhood.

❝ In our daily lives, we are arguably affected the most by local policies, which shape our water access, our streetlights, our K-12 schools, and events like Fourth of July celebrations. Local politics influence what your neighborhood is like and your quality of life.

Adam Dynes

53

The reality is, we are spoiled for voting opportunities. Presidential elections occur every four years. Congressional elections occur every two years, for both the House and Senate (though not all Senators run in each election). On top of that, state elections occur on an almost yearly basis, and so do local elections. Between your Mayor, City Councilmen, Governor, State Legislatures, Sheriff, District Attorney, School Board, Surveyor, Auditor, Treasurer, Senator, Representative, President, etc., you should feel like you have more than enough say in what happens in your community. Still, your voice does not stop there. Most state and local elections let you vote directly on laws, referendums, initiatives, and propositions. You have a real voice and real sway over what happens in America. Don't take that lightly.

Martin Luther King, Jr

Our lives begin to end the day we become silent about things that matter.

Ponder

Ponder

How loud can I make my voice by voting?

If you have more to say, additional space is available at the back of the book.

COMMANDMENT 4

You vote for a representative

COMMANDMENT 4

Prepare

The reason that your vote is your voice is because your representative will act on your behalf. Decisions about legislation like taxes, warfare, regulations, etc. are made by elected representatives. In an election, you are choosing someone who will speak on your behalf in those decisions.

When you vote, you are putting your name in support of a political candidate or legislation. That support should be something that you are proud of. Your name is behind that candidate. When they speak in their office, they, in part, carry your voice. You should never vote out of an obligation to "not have the other guy." You should find the candidate you like, know why you like them, and then vote for them. Let your candidate be the best representative for your voice.

> " If you're blessed enough to serve in public office, then you shouldn't just talk a good game about your values; you should cast your vote according to them.
>
> John Thune

> By definition and title, senators and House members are representatives. This means they are intended to be drawn from local populations around the country so they can speak for and make decisions for those local populations, their constituents, while serving in their respective legislative houses. That is, representation refers to an elected leader's looking out for his or her constituents while carrying out the duties of the office.

SUNY American Government Studies

Does your candidate make you proud? Does your candidate inspire? Would you feel comfortable if your candidate represented you in other capacities?

That is what a political representative does. They stand-in for their constituents. They govern on our behalf. They serve their constituents.

Ponder

How do you want to be represented?

Ponder

If you have more to say, additional space is available at the back of the book.

Precept 5

What if my candidate isn't elected?

Prepare

You vote to put your name behind someone you believe can represent you, but what if that person is not elected? What if the people vote for someone whose views are diametrically opposed to your own? How do you behave?

You certainly are not required to sit and grit your teeth for the next several years until a new voting cycle occurs.

Remember, the person who is elected is elected to represent the entirety of their constituency, not just the people who voted for them. The President represents the entire nation, not just one party. A Senator represents an entire state. A Mayor represents their city, not just their voters. If the person you voted for is not elected, the elected person is still your representative. They are still required to hear your opinions and serve you in the capacity of their office.

The key word for you is "advocate." Very little is accomplished by berating your representative. Advocate. If there are issues that concern you, let your representative know. Call the office of your Senator. Ask to meet with your mayor. Write to the President. When you do, advocate. Especially if you write a letter or make a phone call, politeness and genuine passion for good will go much farther than anger, swear words, and insults.

57

Public offices are beholden to the people. You can hold your representative accountable. They are required to serve you in their office whether you voted for them or not. That doesn't mean that you can demand them to do your whim. It does mean that they will listen to you, help you, and try to serve you.

Pray for and support your representatives. They are there on your behalf. Even if you would never vote for them in a million years, you can still pray that they make wise decisions. You can still petition for redress of grievances. You can always advocate for good. There is no need to tear down. The world has too much of that. Build up. Advocate. Seek to help make the world better, even and especially if the person you voted for does not get elected to office.

> " Ask not what your country can do for you — ask what you can do for your country.

John F. Kennedy

Ponder

What am I an advocate for?

Ponder

If you have more to say, additional space is available at the back of the book.

Proclaim your beliefs about Commandment 4 and voting

Look back at what you have written as you studied Commandment 4.

As you studied, you may have written paragraphs upon paragraphs, a few words, or nothing at all. Whatever you wrote is completely fine. However, right now, we invite you to truly take a moment and proclaim in writing:

What does my vote mean?

Put as much or as little as you like, but put something. Put something that you can say honestly, shamelessly even. It may even be aspirational. That's great! There may be something that you write down that you feel you need to change. That's great too! This is a time to reflect as well as proclaim. Let this be something that guides you.

Then take a few more minutes to ponder any upcoming elections. With the candidates involved, what does your vote mean to them?

Take an honest look. Don't just put down what you want to be true because your emotions about it are heightened or because they are from your political party. Truly and honestly, what does your vote mean to your candidates?

Proclaim

What does my vote mean?

Proclaim

COMMANDMENT 4

60

What does my vote mean to my candidates?

COMMANDMENT 4

Now compare.
How do the candidates match up with your own personal views?
Where are they the same? Where are they different?

COMMANDMENT 4

What my vote means to me

Same

Different

What my vote means to my candidates

Same

Different

If you have more to say, additional space is available at the back of the book.

Commandment 5

"Honor thy father and thy mother"

Principle

You and your candidates have to know the history and the laws surrounding government structure, voting, and your rights

Precepts

1. The three types of government
2. The Articles of Confederation Through the End of Revolutionary War
3. The Articles of Confederation after the Revolutionary War
4. The Constitutional Convention
5. The three branches of government
6. Checks and balances
7. The United States: a democratic republic
8. Congressional representation
9. How the President is elected
10. The Bill of Rights and other amendments
11. Meaningful discussion
12. Consistency and equality toward the law

Prepare

Your heritage helps you to understand who you are. It is your responsibility to do right by your heritage. The best way to do that is to know your heritage, and then improve upon it. You cannot passively honor your father and mother; it takes a clear conscious effort.

For some it may not feel possible to honor your father and mother due to trauma, separation, or other circumstances. That is just fine. This is your opportunity to create a new legacy. One that is in your name, and made by you. While it helps you to know who you are, you are not solely

C
O
M
M
A
N
D
M
E
N
T

5

64

defined by your heritage. What do you want your posterity to be? What do you want them to honor?

As you move forward, recognize both the good and the bad that exists in your personal heritage. Magnify the good, and root out the bad. Don't just ignore the bad. Do what you can to make it right so that the goodness can shine. As you do so, you will feel more complete, and your life will improve.

America's heritage helps us to understand who we are. God (with a capital "G") played a role in creating that heritage, and He wants us to do right by it. America's history is filled with greatness, kindness, service, triumph, and beauty. It also has its ugly moments that we should not shy away from. Ours is to give honor to the nation. The only way we can do that is to know the history and improve upon it. We cannot passively honor America.

We have to know the past, know how we got here, know what makes us, know where we fell short, where we failed to do right by our name. We have to magnify the good and root out the bad. This cannot just be done on a superficial level. It needs to be specific, factual, and actionable. We need to know the history that created the government structure that we have today, what that structure is, and why it was made that way. Specifically, we have to know the Consitution.

This Commandment will be different from the other Commandments. We will examine how America's governance came to be. We will also explore why it is so unique, what its founding principles are, and why those principles are important. This is going to be the longest Commandment in this book. That is by design. It's vital to remind yourself of America's Constitutional history, government structure, and guiding principles. The Fifth Commandment will take you through twelve precepts.

The Precepts will be as follows:
1. The three types of government.
2. The Articles of Confederation. Through the End of Revolutionary War.
3. The Articles of Confederation after the Revolutionary War.

4. The Constitutional Convention.
5. The three branches of government.
6. Checks and balances.
7. The United States: a democratic republic.
8. Congressional representation.
9. How the President is elected.
10. The Bill of Rights and other amendments.
11. Meaningful discussion.
12. Consistency and equality toward the law.

By the end of your study of this Commandment, you will be able to Proclaim, "How do you feel about the Constitution, the government, and voting laws?" We encourage you to focus on this as you study for yourself, as well as ask it of the candidates you are considering voting for.

C
O
M
M
A
N
D
M
E
N
T

5

How do you feel about the Constitution, the government, and voting laws?

"it seems to have been reserved to the people of this country, by their conduct and example, to decide the important question, whether societies of men are really capable or not of establishing good government from reflection and choice, or whether they are forever destined to depend for their political constitutions on accident and force."

Alexander Hamilton

The three types of government

Prepare

There are three basic types of government: monarchies, democracies, and oligarchies. A monarchy is ruled by an individual. A democracy is ruled directly by the people. An oligarchy is ruled by a group of people; an oligarchy is known as a republic when that group of rulers consists of representatives.

Each of the three types of government have benefits and weaknesses. A monarchy is fast-acting, and excels at defense, warfare, and quick-acting legislation, but can lead to a tyrannical dictator. A pure democracy is somewhat fast-acting (though not nearly as fast as a monarchy). It excels at creating laws and governance that directly reflects the will of the people, but can lead to a tyranny under the will of the majority. Democracies are also easily swayed by charismatic and popular figures. An oligarchy is slow-acting, and excels at creating well-studied, well-implemented laws, but is poor at warfare and defense, and can lead to class divide with a ruling elite or aristocracy.

Democracy: Two wolves and a lamb voting on what to have for lunch.

Benjamin Franklin

Nearly every form of government, especially in modern times, has some form of voting system. That voting system may include voting on a candidate, laws, representatives, etc. Most associate voting with votes cast by the people. However, government officials and representatives regularly vote on laws and ordinances. In the United States, the people have some form of vote on most issues, either by electing representatives who vote on their behalf, or by voting for laws directly.

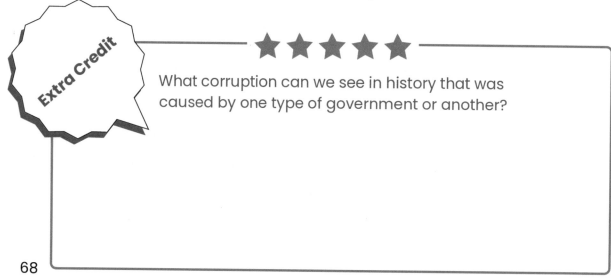

Extra Credit

★ ★ ★ ★ ★

What corruption can we see in history that was caused by one type of government or another?

68

The Articles of Confederation through the end of the Revolutionary War

Prepare

The first time the United States of America really took form, in an official sense, was with the signing of the Declaration of Independence. It's easy to think that, after that, the Revolutionary War was fought, the Constitution was written, and America came to be. But, during the war, something had to keep the nation functioning. Something had to give structure and order to the United States. That "something" was the Articles of Confederation. They were America's first attempt at free government and liberty. They were one of the great founding documents of the United States. The Articles of Confederation walked so that the Constitution could run.

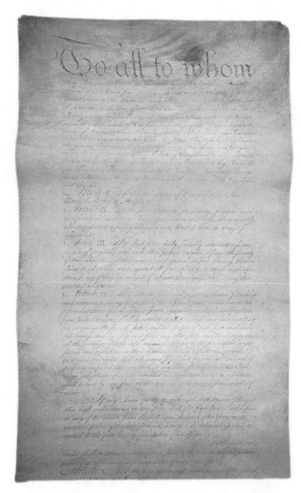

The Articles of Confederation enumerated the governing layout for the Patriots during and just after the Revolutionary War. It's easy to say that the Articles of Confederation were terrible, that they nearly cost us the war, and our independence. To a degree that's true. It had a slow-acting Congress, who had hardly any power to levy taxes. The Congress seemed relatively unconcerned with national security or the Revolutionary War (though, whether that was an issue with the Articles themselves or just the people in Congress at the time is hard to say). Soldiers died from lack of food and supplies. Whole territories were lost because of poor of funding and support.

Still, the Patriots won the war, so the Articles of Confederation did something right. They were drafted in about a year and half, in the middle of the Revolutionary war. They attempted to balance the sovereignty of each state with the unity of the states as a nation. Though mediocre at best, they provided enough strength and supplies for the soldiers to win the war. They even set the backdrop for the Constitution and American success. Without the Articles of Confederation, America would not be here today.

However, at the end of the Revolutionary War, many were unsatisfied. The nation was beyond fragile when the War finished. Revolutionary soldiers were furious. They had fought for years, suffering through heat, sickness, cold, bloody battles, parasites, and all manner of shelters. They hadn't even been paid yet. They had won the liberty of their nation, but for what? The Congress established in the Articles of Confederation didn't seem to care. The soldiers gathered together, and began plotting to overthrow Congress by force.

George Washington heard of their plan, and entered the room; hidden in his pocket was a letter from a sympathetic Congressman. The soldiers were silent. Here he was, Washington himself. The leader of the army. He had carried them to victory. He had been with them every step of the way. No one merited greater respect from these revolutionary soldiers.

"Gentlemen," he said. "An attempt has been made to convene you together—how inconsistent with the rules of propriety! How unmilitary! and how subversive of all order and discipline." In other words, "What are you doing? How could you, after all this, come together to overthrow the very nation you just fought to liberate?"

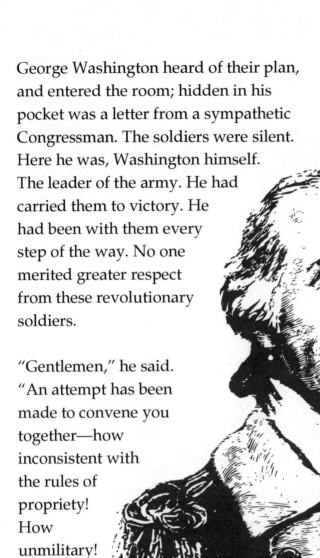

He reached into his pocket and pulled out the letter. He held it close, then far away, then close again, straining to read it. He looked up at the men, paused, and said, "Gentlemen, you will permit me to put on my spectacles, for, I have grown not only gray, but almost blind in the service of my country." This was no small thing. For the first time, Washington allowed himself to be seen as frail, as fallible. This was General Washington, the unkillable man, and he allowed his men to see that his body was beginning to fail him. Washington knew that this was a critical moment. America could not survive through mob rule where might makes right. He read the letter, and ordered the soldiers to stand down.

Still, Washington knew that, to a degree, they were correct. The Congress couldn't stand as it was in the Articles of Confederation. The Articles created a weak legislative body. They were slow acting, poorly funded, and far too distant from the needs of the people. Something had to change.

Federalist Papers

The Insufficiency of the Present Confederation to Preserve the Union

There are material imperfections in our national system...something is necessary to be done to rescue us from impending anarchy...The evils we experience do not proceed from minute or partial imperfections, but from fundamental errors in the structure of the building...Here, my countrymen, impelled by every motive that ought to influence an enlightened people, let us make a firm stand for our safety, our tranquillity, our dignity, our reputation. Let us at last break the fatal charm which has too long seduced us from the paths of felicity and prosperity.

Alexander Hamilton

Extra Credit

★★★★★

What do you think of the Articles of Confederation?

The Articles of Confederation after the Revolutionary War

Prepare

The Articles of Confederation could not levy taxes. All government income came from donations rather than taxes. In 1786, the full federal budget was $3.8 million. That year, they collected $663. Not 663 thousand dollars, not 663 million, 663 total dollars. This was unsustainable. The government could not function this way. How could we be the United States of America, if the uniting, governing body had $663 to its name?

The framers gathered the best minds together to create what we now know as the Constitution. They had to be careful. This would eliminate the government system that had gotten them through the Revolutionary War. Difficult as they were to work with, that Congress helped get it done. Moreover, the framers were about to make a government that had the power to levy taxes, and to enforce those taxes. Taxation was one of the principal issues that led to the Revolutionary War; that, and an overbearing government body. Still, the framers knew that if they took the best parts of governments throughout history and combined them together, the nation would be successful.

It is essential that you should practically bear in mind that towards the payment of debts there must be revenue; that to have revenue there must be taxes; that no taxes can be devised which are not more or less inconvenient and unpleasant.

George Washington

Essentially, they knew that America would need a strong central government, one that was powerful enough to have an army, to levy taxes, to enact law, and to protect the rights and securities of the nation. At the same time, it had to do that without the possibility of becoming corrupt and overstepping its authority.

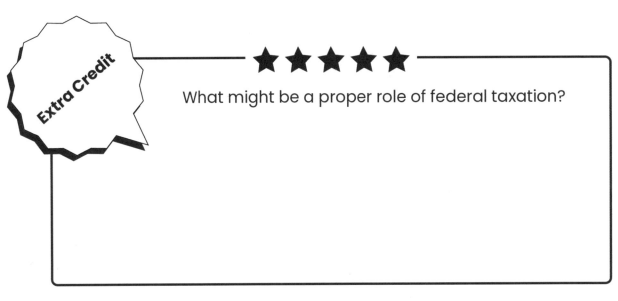

Extra Credit

★★★★★

What might be a proper role of federal taxation?

If you have more to say, additional space is available at the back of the book.

The Constitutional Convention

Prepare

George Washington was unanimously elected to lead the Constitutional Convention. Essentially, he presided at the Convention. Washington rarely spoke and almost never gave his opinion. He knew that he was well respected and well admired. If he spoke up, no one would debate him. Debate, rebuttals, and argument would be the key to success. Washington was to lead and guide rather than decide. With Washington leading, it was time to make the Constitution.

Interestingly, James Madison is considered the father of the Constitution. He was the one who wrote the initial draft of the Constitution. From there he edited it, re-edited it, and eventually drafted the final version that we have today. Madison's work laid America's foundation.

The format and content of the Constitution was hotly debated. The fifty-five delegates argued for four months, meticulously choosing exactly how the nation would run. They knew they had to base the Constitution on eternal truth. How that looked and what that meant was constantly scrutinized. However, with Madison taking the wheel and Washington presiding, the framers made the Constitution. It laid out the basic system of governance that we have in America today.

Ronald Reagan

❝❝ Almost all the world's constitutions are documents in which governments tell the people what their privileges are. Our Constitution is a document in which we the people tell the government what it is allowed to do.

Extra Credit

★★★★★

What makes the United States Constitution unique?

The three branches of government

Prepare

The Constitution designed the government to have three branches, the legislative branch, the executive branch, and the judicial branch.

The legislative branch, known as Congress, has two groups; the House of Representatives, and the Senate. Together, they have the power to draft and enact laws. Furthermore, they can lay and collect taxes; they can borrow money and regulate commerce; they can raise and support armies and navies and can declare war. They also manage the post offices and roads.

The executive branch consists of the President, the Vice President, and the Presidential Cabinet. The President is the Commander in Chief of the armed forces. The President directs the military, and appoints the Vice President and Supreme Court Justices. The President also approves laws that have been passed by the Congress and House of Representatives. The President can veto a law, meaning that that law has been rejected. However the House and Senate can repass the law by a super majority, meaning a ⅔ vote in favor of the bill. The Vice

President ensures the security of the vote, presides over the Senate, and is the next in line for President should the President not be able to serve in office anymore (due to death, conviction after impeachment, etc.). The Cabinet consists of offices of management (the Secretaries of Commerce, Defense, Homeland Security, Energy, etc.). They help manage and oversee their respective aspects of governance.

The judicial branch is the court system of the United States. judicial power rests first in the Supreme Court, and then in the lower courts. The Supreme Court is the highest court in the nation, and has nine judges, called Justices, that preside over it. The supreme court Justices are appointed by the President. They hold the power to examine any law that has passed through Congress. They can determine if that law is constitutional. The Supreme Court also deals with any interstate legal conflicts as well as legal concerns surrounding treaties. The Supreme Court is the least politicized body in the federal government. Contrary to popular belief, the vast majority of their rulings are unanimous or nearly unanimous. Efforts to politicize or pack the courts should be highly scrutinized.

Why is each branch of government important?
Which is most important to you? Why?

If you have more to say, additional space is available at the back of the book.

Checks and balances

Prepare

Madison took the best aspects of each of the three types of government. As we just covered, he organized the government with three distinct branches, the executive branch, the legislative branch, and the judicial branch. He gave aspects of monarchy, oligarchy, and democracy to each one.

The President has the benefits of a monarch. They are fast-acting (what Alexander Hamilton calls "energetic") but are unlikely to become tyrannical because they lack the power to legislate. Congress has the benefits of an oligarchy. They (ideally) create well-examined laws for the benefit of the nation. The power of democracy lies in the hands of the people. They elect the Congress and the President. Those, Congressmen, and even the President, represent the people. Thus, America is considered a democratic republic. We have representatives that the people vote for. Those representatives, in turn, vote on our behalf.

Congress has two legislative bodies, the Senate, and the House of Representatives. The Senate has two representatives per state. The House has a different number of representatives per state; the number is proportionate to the population of each state. The Senate is more like pure oligarchy, with a group of equally powerful representatives. The House has a more democratic form of oligarchy, as it balances representation with population. Both bodies of Congress legislate according to the will of the people while carefully considering and debating the implications of each law. This further balances oligarchy and democracy. Congressional elections are frequent and generally competitive, so Congressmen typically do their best to reflect the will of their constituents.

In this way, the United States gives citizens a powerful voice in the form of a vote. Your vote plays a real and active role in governance of the United States.

Still, Madison wanted to insure that none of the branches became too

Federalist Papers

It may be a reflection on human nature, that such devices [as checks and balances] should be necessary to control the abuses of government.

Madison

powerful. He made the branches interdependent through a system of checks and balances. The legislative branch can make laws, but those laws need to be approved by the President and can be overturned by the Supreme Court. The President is Commander in Chief and controls the armed forces, but Congress declares war. The Supreme Court can overturn law, but they are appointed by the President.

> It is by balancing each of these powers against the other two, that the efforts in human nature toward tyranny can alone be checked and restrained, and any degree of freedom preserved in the Constitution.

John Adams

These checks and balances allow the government to be strong without ever becoming overbearing. The three branches also benefit from their own specific designs without inhibiting the other branches. For example, passing laws is a slow process. It is intentionally slow and reactive so that laws are not passed with impunity and lack of judgment. The laws, ideally, will be well thought out because of the time it takes to pass them. That slowness, however, does not inhibit the President. The executive branch, as mentioned before, is energetic. It is able to make quick, bold decisions because it has few restrictions within its assigned field. When dealing with war and armed forces, slow-moving, reactive action can have deadly results. The energetic executive branch allows for that safety. The judicial branch is a council that is neither too small nor too large. Each Justice has enough influence to have comparable speed to the President, while still having to work in council and direction with the other Justices.

Extra Credit

In what ways are checks and balances still working in our government today? Where have checks and balances been reduced or even abandoned?

The United States: a democratic republic

Prepare

We often refer to the United States as a democracy, but this is inaccurate. The reality is, we live in an oligarchy. We have a democratic vote, but, under the Constitution, the United States government is a republic, which is a form of oligarchy. As much as the three types of government were combined, and as much as we believe that we are a democracy, we have representatives. We are governed by a small group of people. That is a republic, an oligarchy. Rule by a few. In America, there is a "ruling class." Public officials are chosen by the people. While they answer to us, they are a ruling class.

The genius of the American system was the ability to create that ruling class with checks to its power. One check is the Supreme court. Another, less-

discussed but more powerful check, is the vote of the people.

The biggest danger of living in an oligarchy is that the ruling class can continually seize control. Our representatives cannot do that because they have to win the vote. Your vote keeps them in check. Your representatives have to answer to you. However, the less active the voters are, the less our representatives have to answer to the people.

We may define a republic to be ... a government which derives all its powers directly or indirectly from the great body of the people, and is administered by persons holding their offices during pleasure for a limited period, or during good behavior.

James Madison

82

The United States is a democratic republic. Our representatives are elected by the voice of the people. Government officials are not brought to power by some appointing body. The people vote, and the official is chosen. This way, they represent the people as well as possible.

You are an inherent part of our government. You are one of the great checks and balances in the American system. Your vote is your voice, and your vote is your power. We often refer to ourselves as a democracy because we can keep our representatives in check. We call ourselves a democracy because we can vote. Your vote is what keeps our republic in check.

Well Doctor, what have we got? A republic or a monarchy?

A republic, madame. If you can keep it.

Elizabeth Willing Powell

Benjamin Franklin

★ ★ ★ ★ ★

Extra Credit

What is the difference between a democracy and a republic? How is the United States system the best of both?

83

If you have more to say, additional space is available at the back of the book.

Congressional representation

Prepare

Representation in Congress was the largest and most intense debate during the Constitutional Convention. They could not decide if states should be represented by population or completely evenly. Should there be one Congressional body or two? How many people should be in Congress?

James Madison had originally drafted a bicameral (two-bodied) system of legislation, but the way it was drafted seriously favored larger, more populous states. As you can imagine, things got heated. Should there even be two legislative bodies? How many representatives should be in each body? If it was the same number per state, it would give disproportionate power to less populous states because their people would have more say. If it was proportionate to state population, this would give disproportionate power to more populous states because they would have more representatives.

The debate was so heated that they almost decided to cancel the entire Convention over it. Finally Benjamin Franklin stood. He was 81 years old, the oldest man in the room. He had said a few words here or there, but mostly sat in silence. In this moment, however, he gave his longest speech of the Convention.

"In this situation of this Assembly groping as it were in the dark to find political truth...how has it happened, Sir, that we have not hitherto once thought of humbly applying to the Father of lights to illuminate our understandings? In the beginning of the contest with G. Britain, when we were sensible of danger we had daily prayer in this room for the Divine Protection. -- Sir, were heard, Our prayers, and they were graciously answered. All of us who were engaged in the struggle must have observed frequent instances of a Superintending providence in our favor. To that kind providence we owe this happy opportunity of consulting in peace on the means of establishing our future national felicity. And have we now forgotten that powerful friend? Or do we imagine that we no longer need His assistance.

"I have lived, Sir, a long time and the longer I live, the more convincing proofs I see of this truth – that God governs in the affairs of men. And if a sparrow cannot fall to the ground without His notice, is it probable that an empire can rise without His aid? We have been assured, Sir, in the sacred writings that "except the Lord build they labor in vain that build it." I firmly believe this; and I also believe that without His concurring aid we shall succeed in this political building no better than the Builders of Babel...

"I therefore beg leave to move -- that henceforth prayers imploring the assistance of Heaven, and its blessings on our deliberations, be held in this Assembly every morning before we proceed to business."

They implored God for His divine help. Roughly two weeks later, the framers agreed on what is now called the Great Compromise. They decided to have two groups, the House of Representatives and the Senate. The House would have representation based on population, one representative for every 30,000 people. The Senate would have two representatives per state. This bicameral system would allow states with more populations to have more say in the house, without infringing upon smaller states with their representation in the Senate.

Interestingly, the House was originally going to have one representative for every 40,000 people, but George Washington, in one of the only

moments he weighed in on the Convention, said it should be one representative for every 30,000. He thought it dangerous to have a small ratio of Congressmen to population. 140 years later, in 1929, the total number of representatives was capped at 435.

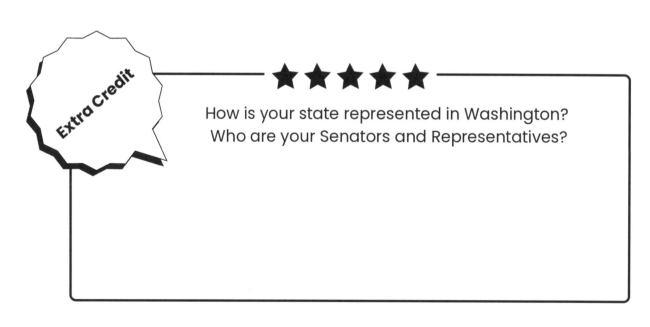

Extra Credit

★★★★★

How is your state represented in Washington?
Who are your Senators and Representatives?

How the President is elected

Prepare

Lastly the framers determined how to vote for the President. They were, initially, going to have the President elected by a true popular vote, where the candidate with the most votes wins the election. However, this would put the Presidential election back in the hands of the majority. That is to say, it brings back one of the pitfalls of true democracy. Instead they decided to use a system of electors and electoral votes. Each state has one electoral vote for every Congressman. This means that each state has a minimum of three electors (two Senators and a minimum

one member of the House of Representatives). The more their population grows, the more Representatives they have in the House. The more Representatives, the more electors.

As the people vote, their votes are counted within their state. Almost every state has a "winner takes all" system. Whichever candidate wins a state's popular vote is awarded all of that state's electoral votes. A candidate needs a majority of the electoral votes, to be elected president. This system allows each state to maintain its sway and influence in the nation while avoiding mob rule in determining the President. Again, the goal was to mitigate any of the negative aspects of one of the three main types of government. Democracy can simply become tyranny under the majority. The electoral system allows the majority to keep significant sway while avoiding the pitfalls of true democracy.

Article II, Section 1, Clause 2

Each State shall appoint, in such Manner as the Legislature thereof may direct, a Number of Electors, equal to the whole Number of Senators and Representatives to which the State may be entitled in the Congress; but no Senator or Representative, or person holding an Office of Trust or Profit under the United States shall be appointed an Elector.

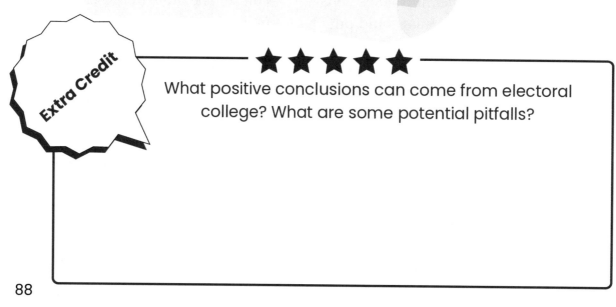

★ ★ ★ ★ ★

Extra Credit

What positive conclusions can come from electoral college? What are some potential pitfalls?

88

If you have more to say, additional space is available at the back of the book.

The Bill of Rights and other amendments

Prepare

When the Constitution was first written, Madison thought it unnecessary to pen a Bill of Rights. He believed it was clear that "the government can only exert the powers specified by the Constitution." However, too many states refused to ratify the Constitution without a Bill of Rights. They wanted assurances that the federal government would not overstep.

There was, once again, serious debate as to what should be included in the Bill of Rights. Madison had just carefully crafted the Constitution.

A process that took argument, debate, planning, prayer, writing, rewriting, and rewriting again. He wasn't about to have someone override that work in a Bill of Rights. So, in 1789, he led the charge in penning the first ten amendments to the Constitution of the United States. We know these as the Bill of Rights.

It's hard to imagine this, but the Bill of Rights was not originally intended to secure rights for individuals, it was meant to curtail the authority of the federal government.

Sure, it says things like "Congress shall make no law regarding…" and "The rights of people…shall not be infringed" and "The rights of people…shall not be violated." But this was with regards to federal actions, infringing on rights, not with regards to rights being untouchable. It's a small distinction but extremely important. It did not secure rights for individuals, it kept the federal government from violating rights.

The importance of that distinction lies in state and local governments. When it was first instituted, state and local governments weren't beholden to the Bill of Rights. They could still make laws about free speech and religion, could still perform unreasonable search and seizure, etc. That would remain the case until after the Civil War.

Congress's biggest power is the power to amend the Constitution. Up to the Civil War, only two amendments had been passed. One clarified boundaries for lawsuits, and one revised and outlined the electoral college in presidential voting.

However, just after the Civil War, Congress passed the two most influential amendments outside of the Bill of Rights. The thirteenth amendment abolished slavery. The fourteenth amendment said, "No State shall make or enforce any law which shall abridge the privileges or immunities of citizens of the United States; nor shall any State deprive any person of life, liberty, or property, without due process of law; nor deny to any person within its jurisdiction the equal protection of the laws." Essentially this was the law that made the Bill of Rights personal. No longer were amendments simply limits on federal power, they were now a guarantee of individual liberties. The 14th amendment is what made the Bill of Rights a personal protection of your liberties.

Your Constitutional rights are protected. Study the Constitution. Study the Bill of Rights. Study the rest of the amendments. Know your rights. They are protected. Know the laws of your land. They are important. Far too many people simply repeat what they see on the news, or social media. Do your own research. Learn your rights. Lean on them. Advocate for your rights. Live them to the fullest extent. Know the law. Advocate for the law. Understand and debate upcoming bills. Contact your representatives. Be active. The laws of the land apply to you, and cannot, legally, infringe on your rights. Check your candidate. Do they openly support and sustain the Constitution and the Bill of Rights?

C
O
M
M
A
N
D
M
E
N
T

5

> **"** The powers delegated by the proposed Constitution to the federal government are few and defined. Those which are to remain in the State governments are numerous and indefinite. **"**

James Madison

★ ★ ★ ★ ★

Extra Credit

Which right, inumerated in the Bill of Rights, do you think is the most importatnt?

Meaningful discussion

Prepare

There are ways and means to express discontent with a law and to go about enacting change. If a candidate and/or politician does not agree with a law, it is both their right and their duty to express that discontent. They should be clear and open about why they do not like a law. They can, then, through proper legal means, seek to change that law. They should also express respect toward Congressional authority. If a law is passed, it is the law. That law deserves respect. If a law ought to be changed or repealed, there are clearly enumerated means to do so.

This is not to say that a candidate should passively bend to the will of the law, and have no concern over what a law says, or how a court interprets it; nor should a candidate be quiet if there is a law they disagree with. They should be willing to challenge and take on damaging or improper laws. They should actively use legal means to push for improvements in the laws of the land. That is one of the great powers and responsibilities of political leaders and something we should seek in our candidates.

Furthermore, a candidate should inspire respect. Candidates should not engage in name-calling, bigotry, unnecessarily aggressive rhetoric, or disrespectful comments. They should treat people with equal respect and dignity.

Great Minds Discuss Ideas. Average Minds Discuss Events. Small Minds Discuss People.

Eleanor Roosevelt

The law sees all as equal. God (with a capital "G") sees all as equal. Eternal truth is the same for one person as it is for the next. A politician's comments should be based on the merits of the issues at hand, not on personal attacks or insults towards individuals or groups.

A candidate should exemplify such character that, if all Americans were to behave and act as they do, we would be a nation of respectful, law-abiding citizens.

Extra Credit

★ ★ ★ ★ ★

What purpose does debate and discussion hold in your life? For the nation? For your candidates?

If you have more to say, additional space is available at the back of the book.

93

Consistency and equality toward the law

Prepare

Consistency toward the law is critical for a candidate. A candidate should respect each law equally. They should not pick and choose which laws they want to respect and not respect. For example, a candidate cannot defend freedom of the press as a critical part of the first amendment, but then turn around and say that freedom to peaceably assemble is not. That is inconsistent. Nor should they say that freedom of the press is critical when it helps them, and then push to limit the press when the press is hurting them. Candidates should consistently sustain the law and have consistent interpretations of the law.

A candidate should not be swayed by monetary influence, political pressure, popularity, etc. They must be firm in their beliefs and understandings.

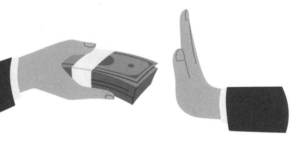

Their knowledge of and commitment to the law is tantamount if they are to participate in the governance of the nation.

> "There can be no truer principle than this—that every individual of the community at large has an equal right to the protection of government."

Alexander Hamilton

Your candidates should always work within legal parameters. There should be no push for extra-legal activity (meaning activity that goes outside of the law). There should be no subversion of the law. They should work within the law to accomplish the ends of their office. There should not be unelected officials who work without accountability to make laws and enforce justice. The law is the law and your candidates should know and sustain it.

Candidates should also respect the rule of law for everyone else. The purpose of liberty and equality is to be equal before the law and the government. The leaders of the nation should hold that equality in high regard. The candidate you vote for should not favor one individual's rights over another. They should not favor one group's rights over another. Leaders should respect equality before the law.

Extra Credit

What can be the danger of elected officials treating people differently under the law?

C O M M A N D M E N T 5

95

Down through history, there have been many revolutions, but virtually all of them only exchanged one set of rulers for another set of rulers. Ours was the only truly philosophical revolution. It declared that government would have only those powers granted to it by the people.

Ronald Reagan

I don't believe in the Constitution because I'm American. I'm American because I believe in the Constitution.

J.S.B. Morse

It's the Bill of Rights that earned America the reputation as the Land of Liberty. The problem is the Bill of Rights is only a document. It doesn't have any magical powers to force government officials to respect it...And that's why if you treasure your freedom, you better elect leaders who are inspired by it and who will wield it to inspire others. Leaders who believe in freedoms and hold the Bill of Rights in reverence.

Robert F. Kennedy Jr.

Proclaim your beliefs about Commandment 5 and voting

Look back at what you have written as you studied Commandment 5.

As you studied, you may have written paragraphs upon paragraphs, a few words, or nothing at all. Whatever you wrote is completely fine. However, right now, we invite you to truly take a moment and proclaim in writing:

How do you feel about the Constitution, the government, and voting laws?

Put as much or as little as you like, but put something. Put something that you can say honestly, shamelessly even. It may even be aspirational. That's great! There may be something that you write down that you feel you need to change. That's great too! This is a time to reflect as well as proclaim. Let this be something that guides you.

Then take a few more minutes to ponder any upcoming elections. With the candidates involved, what are their feelings about the Constitution, the government, and voting laws?

Take an honest look. Don't just put down what you want to be true because your emotions about it are heightened or because they are from your political party. Truly and honestly, how do your candidates feel about the Constitution, Government, and voting laws?

97

What are my feelings about the constitution, the government, and voting laws?

COMMANDMENT 5

If you have more to say, additional space is available at the back of the book.

What are my candidates' feelings about the constitution, the government, and voting laws?

COMMANDMENT 5

Now compare.
How do the candidates match up with your own personal views?
Where are they the same? Where are they different?

COMMANDMENT 5

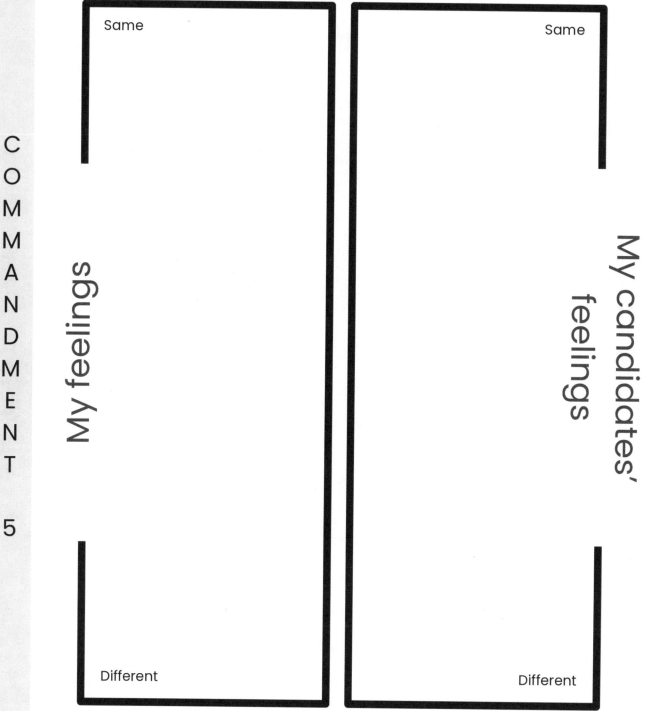

Same

My feelings

Different

Same

My candidates' feelings

Different

Commandment 6

"Thou shalt not kill"

Principle

Everyone has the right to life, liberty, and the pursuit of happiness

Precepts

1. Your candidates should recognize that all are created equal
2. Your candidates should prioritize the rights of American Citizens
3. Your candidates should have clear plans for the interests of non-Americans
4. Your candidates' views on crime and punishment
5. Your candidates' stances on wars

101

Prepare

How do we respect everyone's life, liberty, and right to pursue their own happiness?

The first unalienable right in the Declaration of Independence is the right to life. Plain and simple, your life is yours, and no one else's. But what does life mean? What is its value? Are we allowed to infringe on someone else's life? What does it mean to infringe on someone else's life? Can you forfeit your right to life?

When we are centered on eternal truth, our understanding of life becomes clear. Each person is a living soul with value. That value does not differ from one person to the next. Each person is their own steward. However, we also live in a world of cause and effect, a world of laws. If you let go of an apple, it will fall to the ground. That is the cause and effect of gravity, potential energy, and kinetic energy. There are laws that are always true. For example: an object's inertia is unchanged until acted upon by an outside force; force is equivalent to mass times acceleration; every action has an equal and opposite reaction. Those are Newton's three laws of motion. They are always true. Those laws highlight cause and effect in the universe.

There are also moral laws. That's part of the point of the Ten Commandments. They teach moral law. Much like physical laws, moral laws are always true. When we violate moral laws, there is an effect. When you are unfaithful to your spouse, your spouse is hurt, and you are hurt. When you lie, truth becomes distorted and difficult to understand. Cause and effect. Moral laws are always true and have real, tangible consequences. Moral laws are beholden to cause and effect.

Our government is built on eternal truth and therefore physical and moral laws. When you break those laws there are consequences. Your rights are yours, and your life is yours, and no one can take that away from you. However, your choices are also yours, and the consequences for those choices are something that you have to deal with, both for bad and for good.

For voting, Commandment 6 will take you through five precepts:

1. Your candidates should recognize that all are created equal.
2. Your candidates should prioritize the rights of American Citizens.
3. Your candidates should have clear foreign policies.
4. Your candidates' views on crime and punishment.
5. Your candidates' stances on wars.

By the end of your study of Commandment 6, you will be able to Proclaim, "What does human life mean to you?" We encourage you to focus on this as you study for yourself, as well as ask it of the candidates you are considering voting for.

What does human life mean to you?

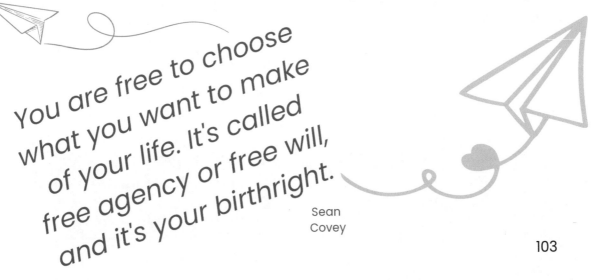

You are free to choose what you want to make of your life. It's called free agency or free will, and it's your birthright.

Sean
Covey

Your candidates should recognize that all are created equal

C
O
M
M
A
N
D
M
E
N
T

6

Prepare

"We hold these truths to be self-evident, that all men are created equal." This is, possibly, the most famous foundational truth of the United States. All are equal, and all are endowed with the same rights. A human life is a human life. We are all children of God. We are all purveyors of eternal truth. Your candidates have to show their belief that all lives are valuable. From the oldest adult to the youngest child.

Regardless of circumstances, no human life is more valuable than another. Irrespective of religion, political affiliation, race, parentage, education, age, sex, addiction, sexual orientation, gender identity, racist ideals, nationality, criminal history, mental capacity, physical capacity, physical development, experience, job, status, income, etc., a human soul is a human soul. From conception to the final heartbeat, a human soul is a human soul, and should be valued as such.

Your candidates should hold your rights in high regard. More importantly they should hold your eternal value in high regard. Human life is sacred. Human liberties are sacred. Human rights are sacred. Of course, the rights, liberties, and protections of an individual can be forfeited by their actions.

> "All mankind... being all equal and independent, no one ought to harm another in his life, health, liberty or possessions."

John Locke

If someone breaks the law and causes harm, that person is guilty and should be prosecuted accordingly (more on that later). However, generally speaking, no action on our part should take away another's rights to life, liberty, and the pursuit of happiness.

Government action should not take away anyone's right to life, liberty, and the pursuit of happiness. Your candidates should not suggest action that takes away an individual's rights. The whole purpose of government is to protect rights. That's why it's there.

Ponder

What does equal mean, what does life mean, and what role does the government have within that?

Ponder

105

If you have more to say, additional space is available at the back of the book.

Your candidates should prioritize the rights of American citizens

Prepare

The United States of America is set up to protect the rights of her citizens. Our laws are written and enumerated. There are checks and balances put in place to protect those rights. The actions of the government cannot infringe upon those rights. Laws cannot violate the Constitution. Your candidates should clearly understand your rights, and know exactly what actions they can take within their role.

Your candidates should also go to great lengths to ensure that their actions will not enable future political figures to infringe upon your rights. The easiest way to do that is to trust that state and local governments will be more successful at legislating than the federal government will. James Madison put it best in the Federalist Papers when he wrote, "**The powers delegated by the proposed Constitution to the federal government are few and defined. Those which are to remain in the state governments are numerous and indefinite.**" At the state level, legislators are much more beholden to their voters. At the local level, voters can often vote for legislation directly. Your candidates should know their place. They are a public servant, whose job is to protect your rights. At the federal level, they should trust the states. At the state and local level, they should listen to their constituents.

> A law is valuable not because it is law, but because there is right in it.

Henry Ward Beecher

Your candidates will also have to navigate issues that do not directly relate to your rights. For example, the President is Commander-in-Chief of the armed forces. A duty which protects your rights by protecting you from outside influences, but, for the most part, does not directly affect your rights. And there's plenty more. After taxes, welfare, regulations, bureaucratic red tape, law-writing, social work, voting, campaigning, debating, casework, training, budgeting, planning, etc. your rights can easily begin to take a back seat. These other responsibilities of your political representatives are extremely important, but they cannot become more important than your protected freedoms. Your rights are a priority.

Ponder

What are the differences between rights, laws, privileges, government benefits, bureaucracy, welfare, etc., and how should they be prioritized?

Ponder

If you have more to say, additional space is available at the back of the book.

Your candidates should have clear plans for the interests of non-Americans

Prepare

A difficult balance with the rights of American citizens is the rights of non-citizens. This includes immigration policies, and foreign policies like trade, tariffs, alliances, intervention, etc. Your candidates should have clear plans for these issues and solutions that can satisfy the ever-globalizing world, without infringing upon American rights, values, and interests. Immigration is an extremely hot-button issue. It can be easy to think of non-citizens as illegal immigrants, but a significant portion of people who enter the United States, attempt to use proper legal processes. Those legal processes are excessively drawn out and have been made even slower by recent legislation. That said, millions of immigrants enter the United States every year, legally and illegally.

How the nation, a state, and/or a local government approach such a massive influx of people can have a serious impact. Over-hostility can snuff out the immense potential of immigrants. If they came to America to become a part of the American dream, why stifle that? However, if laws are too loose and no punishment is affixed, American citizens suffer for it. Rights are infringed upon. Economics, housing, education, cleanliness, infrastructure like waste and sewage management, traffic and civil engineering plans, and even people come under direct threat. Your candidates have to have a clear plan to navigate immigration. They need to address documented and undocumented immigrants, as well as protect American interests.

John F. Kennedy

> Domestic policy can only defeat us; foreign policy can kill us.

Foreign policies, in a general sense, are a federal concern. However, they can have some of the most sweeping and lasting effects of almost any federal policies. Trade deals, tariffs, taxes and regulations affect prices and businesses. Foreign debt can give other nations significant sway over the United States' interests. Foreign intervention can affect international relations and involve the United States in unnecessary conflicts. Alliances and warfare can have an incalculable impact and will be discussed more thoroughly later on. Your candidates should have clearly stated plans for these issues. Their plans should be easy to follow and address the potential outcomes, explaining the benefits and accounting for the pitfalls of those outcomes.

Ponder **Ponder**

What role does the US have in securing rights for non-Americans, and how do we balance American interests?

If you have more to say, additional space is available at the back of the book.

Your candidates' views on crime and punishment

Prepare

Your rights are protected. Those protections take many forms, but the most common one is the rule of law. This nation has laws that everyone has to follow. No individual is above the law. When those laws are violated, there are punishments. Your candidates will have a great deal of sway over the laws that are enacted, the ways they are enforced, and the punishments that are affixed to those laws.

Crime is not a light matter. It should be taken seriously. What actions are criminalized and decriminalized can have immense impact.

This doesn't mean that laws should be tight and strict. Look at alcohol, for instance. It was criminalized in the early 1900s. These stricter laws led to some of the most violent and widespread criminal enterprises in the nation's history. On the other hand, Prop 47, passed in California in 2014, raised the threshold of petty theft to $950 (meaning that an individual could steal that much value and have it be petty theft rather than grand theft. The fine for petty theft is "a fine of not more than $1,000"). This change led to an almost immediate 9% increase in theft in California, with fewer thieves being caught and prosecuted, as the crime was usually not worth the resources for the police and courtrooms. There is no cut and dry answer for crime and punishment. It must be dealt with carefully.

Your candidates should take the issues of crime and punishment seriously. They should make it clear what the crimes are, how they will be punished, and how those punishments will be enforced. Your candidates should have plans for prevention, rehabilitation, and reintegration. Prevention is, usually, more effective than punishment, but your candidates cannot infringe on your rights in the name of justice. Rehabilitation and reintegration should not be throwaway issues and also cannot threaten your rights. Criminals often repeat crimes. Reintegration and rehabilitation are critical for all parties.

When relevant, your candidate's police codes should be clear. Enforcement of laws should not infringe upon Constitutionally

Thomas Szasz

If he who breaks the law is not punished, he who obeys it is cheated.

protected rights.

Your candidates should respect the right to a fair and speedy trial. They should treat everyone fairly before the law. They should not weaponize criminal justice, and use it for personal gain. The law is the law for everyone and should be applied thoughtfully and equally.

Ponder

Ponder

What actions should be criminal, what are the punishments, and how are those crimes enforced?

If you have more to say, additional space is available at the back of the book.

Your candidates' stances on wars

C
O
M
M
A
N
D
M
E
N
T

6

Prepare

War has had more influence over the state of the world than almost any other man-made force. It leads to death, destruction, the movement of people, the acquisition and loss of land, the adjustment of laws, the development of new technologies, the destruction of technologies, the downfall of entire civilizations, the spread of disease, the spread of famine, the creation of businesses, the destruction of businesses, etc. It tears nations and families apart. It enables people to commit unspeakable horrors. It highlights the greatest of individuals in the worst of circumstances. War is sometimes necessary. War is often unnecessary.

Hate multiplies hate, violence multiplies violence, and toughness multiplies toughness in a descending spiral of destruction - - - The chain reaction of evil — must be broken, or we shall be plunged into the dark abyss of annihilation.

Martin Luther King Jr.

Your candidates must be clear on their views of warfare. What do they say of past wars? How do they speak about the Revolutionary War? The Civil War? World War I? World War II? What about the Vietnam War? Or more recent wars like the Gulf War or Iraq and Afghanistan? What do they say of them? What do they believe about America's role in those wars?

What about current and future wars? At the time this book is published Ukraine and Russia are at war. Israel and Palestine are at war. The Myanmar Conflict. China's endless pressure on Taiwan. Not to mention terrorist organizations like Hamas, Al Qaeda, ISIS, JNIM, or Al-Shabaab. The list of warfare could go on indefinitely. What do your candidates think of these issues? What are their plans? What are their preparations for potential future threats?

" **A good king must never seek out war, but must always be ready for it.**

Odin
Maevel's Thor, 2011

We live in a world where entire nations could be decimated in minutes without ever having boots on the ground. Your candidates should have a clear understanding of their role in warfare. The President is the Commander-in-Chief, but Congress declares war. The United States has not officially declared war since World War II. How has that affected our warfare? What do your candidates do to avoid or address the declaration of war? How will your candidates behave if the United States is attacked?

War is an ugly thing, but not the ugliest of things. The decayed and degraded state of moral and patriotic feeling which thinks that nothing is worth war is much worse.

John Stuart Mill

Ponder

Ponder

When and why should America engage in warfare?

If you have more to say, additional space is available at the back of the book.

Proclaim your beliefs about Commandment 6 and voting

Look back at what you have written as you studied Commandment 6

As you studied, you may have written paragraphs upon paragraphs, a few words, or nothing at all. Whatever you wrote is completely fine. However, right now, we invite you to truly take a moment and proclaim in writing:

What does human life mean to you?

Put as much or as little as you like, but put something. Put something that you can say honestly, shamelessly even. It may even be aspirational. That's great! There may be something that you write

down that you feel you need to change. That's great too! This is a time to reflect as well as proclaim. Let this be something that guides you.

Then take a few more minutes to ponder any upcoming elections. With the candidates involved, what does human life mean to them?

Take an honest look. Don't just put down what you want to be true because your emotions about it are heightened or because they are from your political party. Truly and honestly, what does human life mean to your candidates?

What does human life mean to me?

COMMANDMENT 6

If you have more to say, additional space is available at the back of the book.

What does human life mean to my candidates?

If you have more to say, additional space is available at the back of the book.

Now compare.
How do the candidates match up with your own personal views?
Where are they the same? Where are they different?

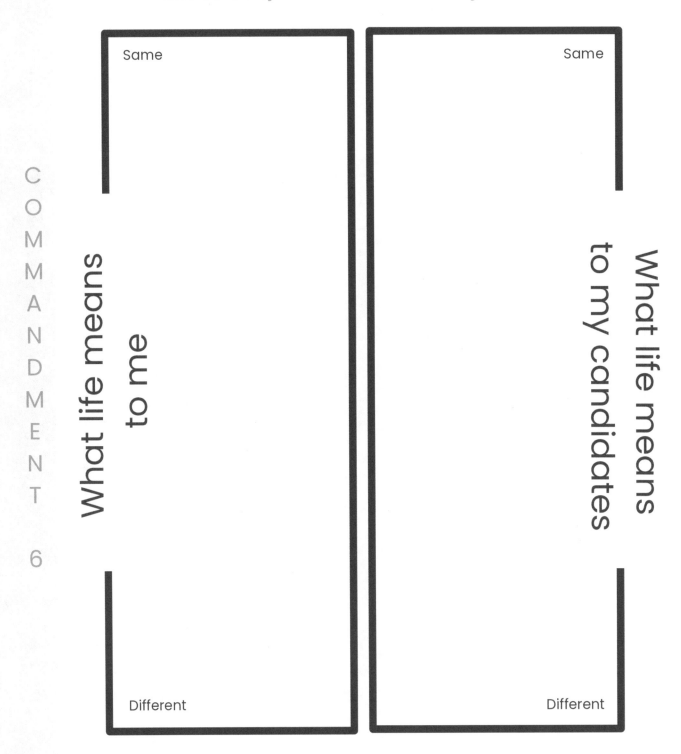

COMMANDMENT 6

What life means to me

Same

Different

What life means to my candidates

Same

Different

If you have more to say, additional space is available at the back of the book.

Commandment 7

"Thou shalt not commit adultery"

Principle

Families are the basic, fundamental, and most important unit of society

Precepts

1. Your candidates' family values
2. Your candidates' views on education
3. Your candidates' views on parental rights

Prepare

How can our governmental system support families?

God cares about families. He could have chosen any title to describe the relationship He has with us. Leader/follower, teacher/student, master/servant. He chose father. He cares about families. He wants us to have a real, tangible connection with

States are called to enact policies promoting the centrality and the integrity of the family.

our families and with Him. Families are the most important relationship in the world. God will not tolerate the destruction of the family.

Our nation should hold the family in the highest regard. The entire sociality

Pope Benedict XVI

120

and structure of our nation is based on the familial core. Family should be protected. It is the most important relationship. Our nation should not abide nor will it survive the destruction of the family. Your candidates should uphold the family as the basic, fundamental, and most important unit of society. They should not be passive regarding family issues.

For voting, Commandment 7 will take you through three precepts:

1. Your candidates' family values.
2. Your candidates' views on education.
3. Your candidates' views on parental rights.

By the end of your study of Commandment 7, you will be able to Proclaim, "What do families mean to you?" We encourage you to focus on this as you study for yourself, as well as ask it of the candidates you are considering voting for.

What do families mean to you?

> **In a world of turmoil and uncertainty, it is more important than ever to make our families the center of our lives and the top of our priorities.**
>
> L. Tom Perry

Precept 1

Your candidates' family values

C O M M A N D M E N T

7

Prepare

Candidates should promote values that support healthy families. They should encourage parents to rear their children in righteousness. This should not merely be done by legislation but by encouragement from your candidates. They should not seek to legislate what families can and cannot do, be, or teach. Families should be protected from government involvement.

Your candidates should promote principles that uphold and support your family. Know for yourself what principles you want your family to have and live. What is your personal identity? What does motherhood mean to you? What does fatherhood mean to you? What does a family look like? What is its structure? Why are these things important to you?

Your candidates should champion principles of love, kindness, patience, education, integrity, fidelity, etc. Living the teachings of your candidates should make your family stronger. How your candidates act should actively and openly strengthen families.

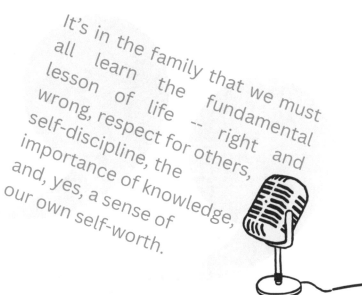

It's in the family that we must all learn the fundamental lesson of life -- right and wrong, respect for others, self-discipline, the importance of knowledge, and, yes, a sense of our own self-worth.

Ronald Reagan

122

> There is no doubt that it is around the family and the home that all the greatest virtues are created, strengthened, and maintained.

Winsotn Churchhill

In promoting a healthy family, your candidates should have a healthy family themselves. They should clearly love and respect their spouse. Their spouse should play an active role in the relationship. They should clearly love their children and their children should love them. As with everything, your candidates should be an example for families to look to and model after.

Your candidates cannot be in support of laws that are destructive to families. Laws that seek to disrupt, dismantle, or even discourage familial ties should be rejected. The Government cannot define what a family looks like, acts like, teaches, or does. The right of parents to raise children how they see fit is as important as any right in the Bill of Rights.

Ponder

Ponder

What are your values with regards to your family?

123

If you have more to say, additional space is available at the back of the book.

Your candidates' views on education

COMMANDMENT 7

Prepare

Education is a family issue. Yes, it happens at school, and yes, curriculums are often handed down by the state, but education is a family matter. What children learn and how they are taught is something that parents get to weigh in on. Your candidates should encourage parental involvement in education.

The idea that education directly involves family is not a new concept. This is well ingrained in the history and tradition of the United States.

The 1925 Supreme Court case of Pierce v. Society of Sisters ruled that:

The fundamental theory of liberty upon which all governments of the Union rest excludes any general power of the State to standardize its children by forcing them to accept instruction from public teachers only. The child is not the mere creature of the State; those who nurture him and direct his destiny have the right, coupled with the high duty, to recognize and prepare him for additional obligations...parents and guardians [have the right] to direct the upbringing and education of children under their control: as often heretofore pointed out, rights guaranteed by the Constitution may not be abridged by legislation.

The right to direct education does not reside in the state. It resides with parents.

> **"** Education begins at home and I applaud the parents who recognize that they - not someone else - must take responsibility to assure that their children are well educated.
>
> Ernest Istook

Your candidates cannot allow the state to take that right away from you. They cannot give schools the power to raise children. Schools should not be allowed to hide things from parents. Parents should be regularly notified of curriculums, events, major life decisions, etc. that children make. Your candidates should trust that parents will act in their child's best interest.

When it comes to education, your candidates should trust families.

COMMANDMENT 7

Ponder

Ponder

What role does the State have in education?

If you have more to say, additional space is available at the back of the book.

Your candidates' views on parental rights

Prepare

Parental rights are rights that parents have by virtue of being parents. It is a natural right. Since its founding the United States has recognized the key role that families and parents take in developing the nation. Your candidates should hold parental rights in high regard.

"The foundations of national morality must be laid in private families."

John Adams

"My mother was the most beautiful woman I ever saw. I attribute my success in life to the moral, intellectual, and physical education I received from her."

George Washington

"All that I am, or hope to be, I owe to my angel mother."

126

Abraham Lincoln

Families don't need meddling. Of course there should be laws that protect families when something is seriously wrong, but those laws should not come at the expense of parental rights. Your candidates should champion parents and encourage parents to take an active role in their children's lives.

From the beginning, the United States has attempted to set up a government that secures rights, not limits them.

When it comes to family, the role of governments is to secure rights and protect freedoms.

Families are where it all happens. Families educate their children. They pass down culture and values. They create great people. Almost any great thing that happens, happens first, most importantly, and most effectively in the family. Your candidates should know that parents do not need regulation. Parents have rights, and those rights should be secure.

Declaration of Independence

To secure these rights, governments are instituted among men, deriving their just powers from the consent of the governed.

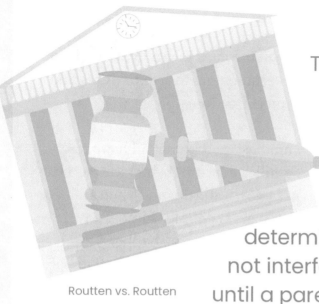

Routten vs. Routten

This Court has determined that parents have a fundamental right to direct the care, custody, and control of their children. This Court also has determined that the government shall not interfere with this right unless and until a parent is proven unfit.

Rights are inexorably linked to corresponding responsibilities. This precept has been about parental rights, what they are, and what they mean. With those rights comes the responsibility to do well as a parent. In seeking to secure parental rights, your candidates should encourage families to take ownership of those rights. They should model and teach proper family values. They should promote love, compassion, forgiveness, and encouragement from parents. They should teach correct principles and let your family govern itself. Your candidates should trust that families are given of God, and that He will bless them.

Ponder

Ponder

What role does the State have in raising children?

If you have more to say, additional space is available at the back of the book.

Proclaim your beliefs about Commandment 7 and voting

Look back at what you have written as you studied Commandment 7

As you studied, you may have written paragraphs upon paragraphs, a few words, or nothing at all. Whatever you wrote is completely fine. However, right now, we invite you to truly take a moment and proclaim in writing:

What do families mean to you?

Put as much or as little as you like, but put something. Put something that you can say honestly, shamelessly even. It may even be aspirational. That's great! There may be something that you write

down that you feel you need to change. That's great too! This is a time to reflect as well as proclaim. Let this be something that guides you.

Then take a few more minutes to ponder any upcoming elections. With the candidates involved, what do families mean to them?

Take an honest look. Don't just put down what you want to be true because your emotions about it are heightened or because they are from your political party. Truly and honestly, what do families mean to your candidates?

What does family mean to me?

COMMANDMENT 7

If you have more to say, additional space is available at the back of the book.

What does family mean to my candidates?

If you have more to say, additional space is available at the back of the book.

Now compare.
How do the candidates match up with your own personal views?
Where are they the same? Where are they different?

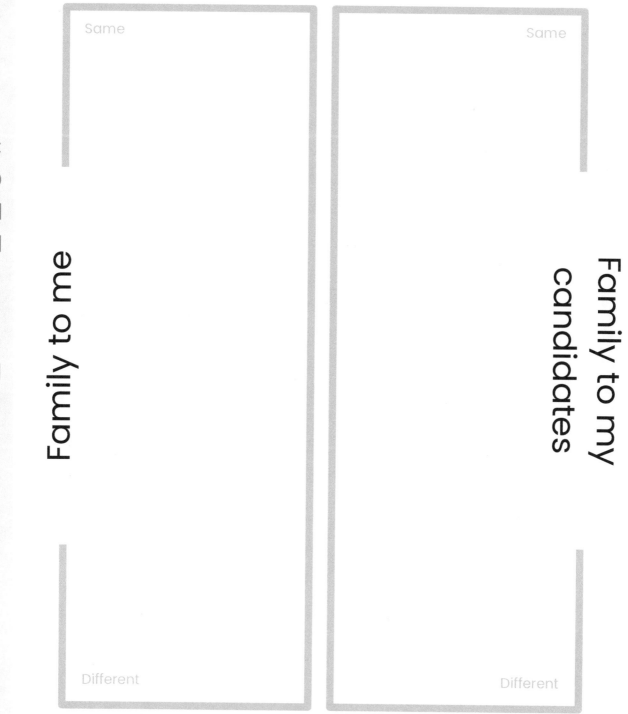

COMMANDMENT 7

Family to me

Family to my candidates

Same

Same

Different

Different

If you have more to say, additional space is available at the back of the book.

Commandment 8

"Thou shalt not steal"

Principle

Economics

Precepts

1. Your candidates should support the free market
2. Your candidates should treat America as the economic superpower
3. Your candidates should have a clear budget to handle economic issues
4. Taxes
5. Your candidates should support and help small businesses
6. Your candidates should encourage charitable giving

133

How do economics impact life, liberty, and the pursuit of happiness?

COMMANDMENT 8

One of the building blocks of eternal truth is that people have stewardship, that is to say, ownership and dominion. When we are faithful over a few things we prepare to rule over many things. Stealing and improper exercise of our stewardship stifles this growth. It shows that we do not value the things God has given to us nor that which has been given to others.

> When you run in debt, you give to another power over your liberty.

Benjamin Franklin

Our nation and economy allows people to be free stewards over their goods. The phrase "life, liberty, and the pursuit of happiness" is based on a statement by John Locke, "life, liberty, and property." Part of our pursuit of happiness is in our ability to own property and have stewardship over that property.

The way your candidates view the economy reflects the way they view stewardship and eternal truth. Stealing and improper exercise of stewardship damages the nation. When improper stewardship or even stealing comes from the government, the national damage increases. When proper morals and good economic practices are put in place, national prosperity increases. America has long been the world leader in technological advancement and economic prosperity. Political leaders should bolster that strength and advance the economy.

For voting, Commandment 8 will take you through 6 precepts:

1. Your candidates should support the free market.
2. Your candidates should treat America as the economic superpower.
3. Your candidates should have a clear budget to handle economic issues.
4. Taxes.
5. Your candidates should support and help small businesses.
6. Your candidates should encourage charitable giving.

By the end of your study of Commandment 8, you will be able to Proclaim, "How do you manage your economics?" We encourage you to focus on this as you study for yourself, as well as ask it of the candidates you are considering voting for.

"How do you manage your economics?"

> If we can but prevent the government from wasting the labours of the people, under the pretense of taking care of them, they must become happy.

Thomas Jefferson

Your candidates should support the free market

Prepare

Markets, typically, function using money. Money is used as a generalized way to measure the value of a good or service. Everything has some sort of value. A decent salad has value. It has less value than a sirloin steak, but more value than fast-food fries. The prices of each item reflect that value, with a salad being cheaper than a steak but more expensive than fries.

When you work, you are generating value. You are compensated for that value with money, which you can then spend for goods and services. Money is a way to conveniently measure value. The economy, at its core, is the widespread exchange of goods, and services, often using money to measure the values of those goods and services.

In a free market, the government does not intervene to try and control the value of money, how much money everyone has, nor how that money has to be spent, either by consumers or companies. A free market trusts that people will, generally, choose goodness. It gives space for people to exercise their own stewardship, for better or for worse. It is built on faith in humanity which fosters growth and innovation.

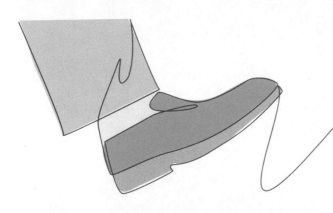

In a controlled market, the government regularly intervenes to define the market standard. The government controls the value of money, how much money people and industries have, and how those people and industries spend their money. A controlled market believes that people will, generally, choose unrighteousness. To prevent people from making poor decisions, it eliminates the opportunity for people to exercise their own stewardship. It puts the definition of goodness and the power of stewardship over money in the hands of a ruling body who defines the market. It is built on distrust of humanity, which stifles growth and innovation.

Find a candidate who trusts the market, who recognizes that the market naturally adjusts itself. The economy does not need the government to force change. Your candidates should regularly express and show faith that positive change will happen.

Let's examine minimum wage. The market naturally takes care of minimum wage issues. For example, most entry-level McDonald's employees earn over $11 per hour. Amazon pays their base employees $15 per hour. Small businesses have similar entry-level pay just to compete in the market. That did not happen because of the government. That happened because the market demanded it.

The real minimum wage is always zero, regardless of the laws, and that is the wage that many workers receive in the wake of the creation or escalation of a government-mandated minimum wage, because they lose their jobs or fail to find jobs when they enter the labor force.

Thomas Sowell

The only way that has ever been discovered to have a lot of people cooperate together voluntarily is through the free market. And that's why it's so essential to preserving individual freedom.

Milton Friedman

C O M M A N D M E N T

8

For your candidates to show trust in the market, they should demonstrate a basic knowledge of markets. They should not simply say buzz-terms and fluffy sayings that sound good but have no substance. They should have a clear understanding of what their fiscal policies are, what those policies will do to benefit the economy, the potential damages the policies might have, and ways to mitigate those damages. Their fiscal policies should have real, articulable results that are proven through history and practice. They should make clear and easily understood assertions about the economy.

Your candidates should inspire people. They should help bolster the American dream. Through smart practice and hard work, anyone can be successful. They should trust the market to make that success. They should trust people to find that success. True success is not found by handouts. Handouts make people rely on government and stifle market growth. True economic prosperity is found in free markets.

Ponder

Ponder

Do you trust the market?

If you have more to say, additional space is available at the back of the book.

Your candidates should treat America as the economic superpower

Prepare

America is the world superpower. We have one of the most active markets. We have the largest companies, the greatest technological innovation, the most powerful army, some of the highest imports and exports, and one of the most influential economies in the world. America's actions direct the world's actions. America's economy directs the world's economy.

Far too often, economic policies force industries overseas. Corporate taxes, minimum wages, trade embargoes, tariffs, free trade agreements, etc. push companies into other nations. Companies often find that they are better off importing their products from China, Mexico, South America, etc. rather than producing their products in America.

Thoughtless economic policies can cause serious damage. They hurt, both America's economy and the world economy at large.

Candidates need to respect the influence of America. Rather than ignoring it, belittling it, or saying it's a bad thing, your candidates should face America's influence head on. The fact that America is a superpower is a good thing. It provides great opportunities for Ameircans, and great opportunities to bless the world. The dollar is the world currency standard for a reason. The power of the dollar and the American economy can and should make the world a better place.

> **The founding generation would be amazed. It would be surprised. I think it would be very impressed by what has happened since then in terms of our exploding population; in terms of the success of this country economically and otherwise.**
>
> Mike Lee

Ponder

Ponder

What are your international economic views?

If you have more to say, additional space is available at the back of the book.

Your candidates should have a clear budget to handle economic issues

Prepare

Your candidates should recognize spending and deficit issues. America is over 35 trillion dollars in debt (at the time this book was written). That is over $100,000 per citizen, not per taxpayer, per citizen, and that is just at the federal level. Politicians need to work toward some level of normalcy on this increasingly unstable deficit. We cannot afford more unfunded spending. We cannot afford more debt. Candidates need to provide a clear and non-destructive plan that says where the money will come from, and what that money will be spent on.

> Many a man thinks he is buying pleasure, when he's really selling himself to it.
>
> Benjamin Franklin

As of the date of writing this, America has been in a period of debt suspension for over a year and a half. There has been no budget. Calls for a budget have been ignored. Spending has gone unchecked. Debt is mounting. Welfare is increasing. The situation is unstable.

Just the interest payments on American debt is approaching 900 billion dollars every year. Budget, on a local, state, and national level is not something to take lightly. Taxpayer money should be spent carefully, consciously, and wisely.

COMMANDMENT 8

> We must not let our rulers load us with perpetual debt...
> It is incumbent on every generation to pay its own debts as it goes. A principle which, if acted on, would save one half the wars of the world.

Thomas Jefferson

Ponder

Ponder

What are valid reasons for America to go into debt?

If you have more to say, additional space is available at the back of the book.

Taxes

Prepare

Hand in hand with budgets and debt is taxes. Tax plans should be clear. What are the candidates going to tax? How much? Why have they chosen those taxes? What will it be spent on? Why is that important? There isn't much more to say about this. Your candidates should make that apparent, and you should, generally speaking, agree with them.

Taxes are not a superficial thing. They are at the core of the foundation of America. "No taxation without representation." Taxes should not be levied lightly, nor should they be spent lightly.

Your candidates should understand taxes. They should be able to tell you the difference between a direct tax (which must be taxed equally amongst everyone) and an indirect tax (which can be taxed unequally). They should be able to tell you the differences and uses of income tax, property tax, capital gains tax, welfare taxes, Social Security tax, etc. They should be able to explain the effects of interest rates. They should understand inflation and how they plan to handle inflation. They shouldn't just tell you what the results will be of their taxes, but why those results will happen.

Most importantly, your candidates should understand that they need to stay in their lane. At the federal level, the power to levy taxes is clearly given to Congress. Congress, alone has that right. Huge portions of legislative power have been handed to the executive branch through the cabinet. Congress does have the authority to appropriate and delegate powers to other entities. But be aware, those entities are members of the presidential cabinet, who are unelected and unaccountable to your vote. This should be clear. If Congress is not controlling taxes, then taxes are probably controlled by people who are not accountable to your vote.

> "You can't tax your way to a balanced budget without tanking the job creation that actually generates tax receipts.
>
> Matt Kibbe

At the state level, governors are regularly increasing their hold over tax plans and legislations. Make sure that your candidates understand their responsibilities and trust other politicians to act on their responsibilities. Don't let your candidates usurp that power for themselves.

I cannot undertake to lay my finger on that article of the Constitution which granted a right to Congress of expending, on objects of benevolence, the money of their constituents.

James Madison

When your candidates are expressing potential taxes, you can ask yourself, "What are these taxes going to? Would that be more adequately accomplished in the private sector?" Surprisingly, only about 20-30 percent of federal money actually reaches its intended destination. There are so many lines of red tape, so many addendums to budget, so much scope-creep to projects, that the actual target only gets 20-30 percent of its intended money. In the private sector, that number ranges from 70-90 percent reaching its target. So, generally speaking, tax plans won't be necessary. If your candidates propose increased taxes, figure out why that task couldn't be done in the private sector.

Ponder

What taxes are necessary, and what taxes are unnecessary?

Ponder

If you have more to say, additional space is available at the back of the book.

Your candidates should support and help small businesses

C
O
M
M
A
N
D
M
E
N
T

8

Prepare

One of the most notable factors of an effective politician is their ability to "generate jobs." Jobs are generated by economic principles that allow companies to grow and lower barriers to entry. Over 60% of new jobs are created by small businesses. Small businesses are also the epicenter for innovation and progress. These small businesses need a liberated market to thrive. Burdensome regulations, unrealistic environmental standards, heavy taxes, labor laws, etc. stifle small businesses. Under those circumstances, it is much harder to grow and create new jobs.

"Starting your own business is one of the most empowering steps you can take in your life. When you launch a business, you're expanding your options for financial freedom so you can pursue even bigger dreams down the road.

Tony Robbins

146

Your candidates should rarely, if ever, propose regulations, laws, or parameters that a company has to meet. Chances are those will almost always do more harm than good. Let's examine two examples.

To combat poverty, people tend to suggest raising the minimum wage. Interestingly a high minimum wage bars people from entering the job market. When the minimum wage is raised, employers hire with increased discrimination. This is devastating to people with GEDs, part-time employees, college students, single parents, people with mental health concerns, people who don't "dress properly," people with tattoos, people with visible scars etc. These should rarely, if ever, play a role in employment, but a higher minimum wage automatically makes these more of a barrier.

Often environmental regulations are intended to manage larger companies. The people who urge these types of regulations often see these large corporations as the enemy. Interestingly enough, those larger companies will happily endure strict environmental regulations if it means that small businesses will rise more slowly. Small businesses lead to increased competition. For example, tech companies like Apple, Intel, Meta, Google, etc. can easily address regulations like emissions limits because they can afford to spend money to bring down their level of emissions or simply pay the fine. While new tech start-ups would be crippled by such regulations and fines. These large tech companies don't want a new company to break into the market, so they will happily deal with the regulations to keep competition at bay.

Regulations and minimum wage laws are just two examples of ways that small businesses are hurt by excessive governmental involvement. Do research to understand candidates' economic plans, and learn what their plans will do to the economy. Don't just base your research on one or two articles.

Conduct thorough, fact-based research. Study historical trends. Study the effects of these kinds of policies in other nations or on a state or city level. Study economic success under your candidates in past years, if such evidence exists. Your candidates should be aware of the potential pitfalls of their policies and should be ready to address them.

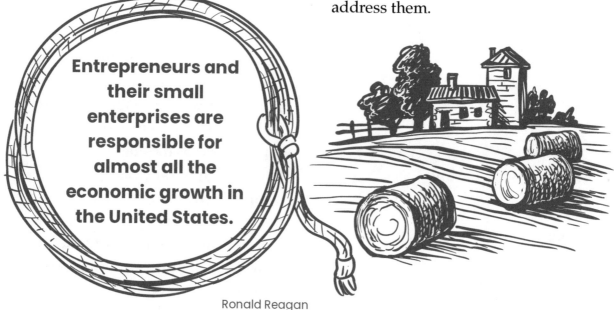

Entrepreneurs and their small enterprises are responsible for almost all the economic growth in the United States.

Ronald Reagan

Ponder

Ponder

What are your candidates' policies that affect businesses, and how, specifically, do they affect small businesses?

If you have more to say, additional space is available at the back of the book.

Your candidates should encourage charitable giving

Prepare

Your candidates should regularly encourage and engage in charity. Private charities, donations, volunteering, etc, are some of the most powerful forces for economic good. Candidates should help America to see the benefit of charitable giving. You should feel inspired to love and help your neighbor.

Taxes, government spending, and welfare programs are highly inefficient. As mentioned before, after layers upon layers of bureaucracy, the misappropriated funds, the unending paperwork, etc., only about 20-30 percent of federal welfare money actually reaches the people who need it. For every $100 spent on welfare, only $30 lands in the pockets of the people who it was meant to help. Let's put that a different way. For every $100 received in welfare, the American taxpayers paid $500. The private sector, especially charities, average between 70% and 90% reaching the final target, making them a far better choice.

Furthermore, charities almost always help people become self-sufficient. They know the circumstances of the local area they serve; they know the people; and they know how best to help. They also rarely have people who remain constantly dependent. Charities help people get on their feet and eventually walk on their own. On the other hand, government welfare tends to lead to increased dependence. People are on government support for years, if not, decades. Welfare creates dependency.

If there was sufficient charitable giving, welfare would not be necessary, taxes would be lower, and the economy would thrive for it. Goodness will go much farther than laws and regulations. Government welfare is, essentially, a forced charity that is not even half as effective. Your candidates should promote goodness long before they promote government welfare.

"We make a living by what we get, but we make a life by what we give."

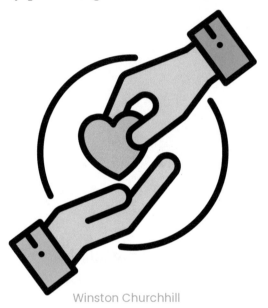

Winston Churchhill

Ponder

What good have you seen come from charitable giving?

Ponder

If you have more to say, additional space is available at the back of the book.

Proclaim your beliefs about Commandment 8 and voting

Look back at what you have written as you studied Commandment 8

As you studied, you may have written paragraphs upon paragraphs, a few words, or nothing at all. Whatever you wrote is completely fine. However, right now, we invite you to truly take a moment and proclaim in writing:

How do you manage your economics?

Put as much or as little as you like, but put something. Put something that you can say honestly, shamelessly even. It may even be aspirational. That's great! There may be something that you write down that you feel you need to change. That's great too! This is a time to reflect as well as proclaim. Let this be something that guides you.

Then take a few more minutes to ponder any upcoming elections. With the candidates involved, how do they manage economics?

Take an honest look. Don't just put down what you want to be true because your emotions about it are heightened or because they are from your political party. Truly and honestly, how do your candidates manage economics?

151

How do I manage my economics?

If you have more to say, additional space is available at the back of the book.

How do my candidates manage economics?

COMMANDMENT 8

If you have more to say, additional space is available at the back of the book.

Now compare.
How do the candidates match up with your own personal views?
Where are they the same? Where are they different?

COMMANDMENT 8

My economics

My candidates' economics

Same

Same

Different

Different

If you have more to say, additional space is available at the back of the book.

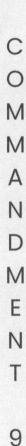

Commandment 9

"Thou shalt not bear false witness"

Principle

Honesty

Precepts

1. Your candidates should avoid the three types of lies
2. Your candidates should respect the value of information
3. Your candidates should represent the level of honesty that you hope to display

Is there any such thing as an honest candidate?

COMMANDMENT 9

God (capital "G") knows all things. The other way this program refers to god is eternal truth. We have to center on truth. Dishonesty is, inherently, not truthful. To bear false witness, to lie, is to make a mockery of truth. Choose to be honest, to have integrity. Center on eternal truth.

Biblically speaking, we will be judged of God.

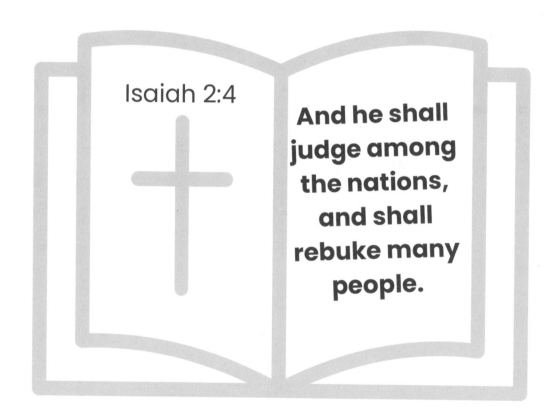

Isaiah 2:4

And he shall judge among the nations, and shall rebuke many people.

Are we an honest nation? Do we have integrity? Honesty and integrity will protect America and lead her to greater prosperity. The integrity of this nation is linked to the integrity of her political figures. Your candidates should be honest. The offices to which they are appointed require honesty.

For voting, Commandment 9 will take you through three precepts:

1. Your candidates should avoid the three types of lies.
2. Your candidates should respect the value of information.
3. Your candidates should represent the level of honesty that you hope to display.

By the end of your study of Commandment 9, you will be able to Proclaim, "Are you honest?" We encourage you to focus on this as you study for yourself, as well as ask it of the candidates you are considering voting for.

Are you honest?

Abraham Lincoln

66 I am a firm believer in the people. If given the truth, they can be depended upon to meet any national crisis. The great point is to bring them the real facts. 99

66 The whole art of government consists in the art of being honest. 99

Thomas Jefferson

Your candidates should avoid the three types of lies

COMMANDMENT 9

Prepare

Candidates should be honest. This is already a big ask. Chances are, your candidates have been dishonest about something at some point. Keep in mind, though, so has everyone. This is not about perfection, this is about intent. Are your candidates trying to mislead you? Are they trying to be honest? Are their motives honest and pure? Are their policies backed by their beliefs? Do they follow through on their promises? How often are they dishonest?

> Honesty is more than not lying. It is **truth** telling, **truth** speaking, **truth** living, and **truth** loving.
>
> James E. Faust

The easiest way to know if your candidates are honest is to look for the lies they tell and the way they tell them. There are three main types of lies, commission, omission, and paltering.

Commission is the most obvious type of lie. This occurs by making up false information. For example, a child at the store calls her mother and asks if she can buy a toy. Her mom says that she can't. The girl then tells her dad, "I called mom and she said that you have to buy me a toy." The daughter is making up that information. That is a lie of commission.

Omission is a less obvious lie. It is leaving out information in a way that is misleading.

If, in that same situation, the daughter told her dad, "We should buy a toy. I just called mom about it." She has left out some critical information, which is, Mom said not to buy a toy. She didn't make up any information, but she left out information in such a way that it tells a completely different story.

Paltering is not as common of a lie, but it can be the most cunning. Paltering is using a series of truthful statements to say something false.

For example, the daughter might have gotten permission from her mom to buy a toy last month, but when she called today, her mom didn't give permission. She could still go to her dad and say two truthful statements that lead to a lie. "Mom said I could buy a toy (true). I just called her (true)." Both of those are true statements, but, in sequence, make a lie.

While these examples are a bit silly and simple, they help illuminate the different types of lies. Generally, candidates will tell lies of commission and omission. They will make up information and statistics that support their campaigns, or they will twist information to their benefit, attributing successes or failures to various policies and omitting the real cause. Paltering is more common in writings, op-eds, and political advertising but less common in speeches, debates, and interviews.

Your candidates will never be fully honest, but they will have tendencies. Watch your candidates. What are their trends? What are their lifestyles? How do they lie? And how often?

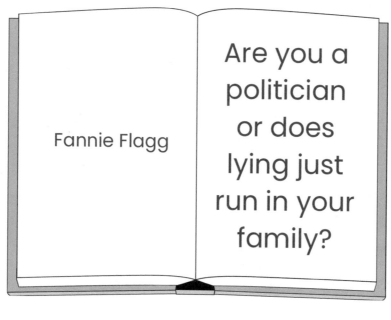

Fannie Flagg

Are you a politician or does lying just run in your family?

Ponder

Ponder

How do you lie?

If you have more to say, additional space is available at the back of the book.

Your candidates should respect the value of information

Prepare

Information and understanding is one of the most valuable things that we have access to. Government leaders have immense control over the flow of information and the public response to that information. America's vast access to information is too grand for dishonest hands.

How does a country ensure checks and balances on truth? How do you as a citizen ensure that information is protected and accessible? Find a candidate that respects the first amendment. You have freedom of the press, freedom of speech, freedom of information. You are entitled to truth. In fact, you are supposed to center your life on it.

That may be the best check for the way your candidates will treat information. What are the truths they center their lives on? If they center on great eternal truths, they will hold truth and information in high regard, and do their best to disseminate it quickly and accurately. If they are not well centered, they will not respect truth. They will not respect your rights.

Furthermore, politicians (especially the President) are entrusted with the nation's most important secrets. Like all nations, the government has secrets, operations, projects, etc. that are kept as objects of national security. Elected officials need to deal honestly with those secrets. Candidates and political leaders cannot deal lightly with these issues; they cannot be loose in their portrayal of truth; they cannot treat our nation's integrity as a small thing.

Lastly, political leaders rarely, if ever, deal in small amounts. Even at the local and state level they deal on scales of thousands, millions, and even billions of dollars. At the federal level they sometimes deal in trillions of dollars. The federal government also controls the most powerful army in the world. They declare war, engage the military, allocate funds, negotiate trade regulations, enforce and enact law, etc. Why would you entrust that to someone dishonest? To deal on such a scale, your candidates must be of uncompromising integrity.

George Orwell

" Who **controls** the past controls the future. Who **controls** the present **controls** the past.

Ponder

Ponder

How do you want information to be handled/controlled, and who should handle/control it?

If you have more to say, additional space is available at the back of the book.

Precept 3

Your candidates should represent the level of honesty that you hope to display

Prepare

As discussed earlier, America is a republic. This means that our elected officials represent the people. The characteristics of elected officials reflect the characteristics of Americans. We choose our leaders. If the president is dishonest, Americans are seen as dishonest.

In our elections, we choose who represents us. America is great because Americans are good. Our elected officials must reflect that goodness. Once again, politicians should be an example to the people. Our president should be the ultimate example of American honesty, kindness, and steadfastness.

If the people elect a dishonest person, they are, in essence, saying that they are okay with dishonesty, that they trust a dishonest person to represent them properly.

❝❝Honesty is the best policy.

Benjamin Franklin

163

Honesty should be ingrained in the lifeblood of America. One of the most famous folktales about George Washington comes from when he was a boy. He cut down the cherry tree, and when his father asked what happened he said, "I cannot tell a lie." He was an example to the nation. That level of honesty and integrity should be hallmarks of worthy candidates.

Frederick Douglass

The life of the nation is secure only while the nation is **honest**, **truthful**, and **virtuous**.

Ponder

Ponder

How do your candidates and representatives reflect your inegrity?

164   If you have more to say, additional space is available at the back of the book.

Proclaim your beliefs about Commandment 9 and voting

Look back at what you have written as you studied Commandment 9

As you studied, you may have written paragraphs upon paragraphs, a few words, or nothing at all. Whatever you wrote is completely fine. However, right now, we invite you to truly take a moment and proclaim in writing:

Are you honest?

Put as much or as little as you like, but put something. Put something that you can say honestly, shamelessly even. It may even be aspirational. That's great! There may be something that you write down that you feel you need to change. That's great too! This is a time to reflect as well as proclaim. Let this be something that guides you.

Then take a few more minutes to ponder any upcoming elections. With the candidates involved, are they honest?

Don't just put down what you want to be true because your emotions about it are heightened or because they are from your political party. Truly, are your candidates honest?

165

Proclaim

Am I honest?

COMMANDMENT 9

If you have more to say, additional space is available at the back of the book.

Are my candidates honest?

COMMANDMENT 9

167

If you have more to say, additional space is available at the back of the book.

Now compare.
How do the candidates match up with your own personal views?
Where are they the same? Where are they different?

My integrity

My candidates' integrity

Same

Same

Different

Different

If you have more to say, additional space is available at the back of the book.

Commandment 10

"Thou shalt not covet"

Principle

Happiness

Precepts

1. Happiness is infinite
2. Happiness comes from agency paired with righteousness
3. "Privilege" is a principle of oppression
4. Socialism is inherently covetous
5. Build your own happiness

MomSquad

Happiness is eternal. It is the result of centering your life on God, on eternal truth. The purpose of America, from its foundation, is to form a government and a nation that allows the greatest potential happiness. These immortal lines from the Declaration of Independence would be enough to prove that America's purpose is happiness:

C O M M A N D M E N T 10

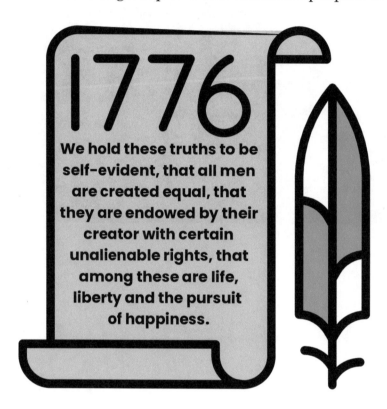

1776

We hold these truths to be self-evident, that all men are created equal, that they are endowed by their creator with certain unalienable rights, that among these are life, liberty and the pursuit of happiness.

But that great founding document does not stop there:

To secure these rights, Governments are instituted among Men, deriving their just powers from the consent of the governed, – That whenever any Form of Government becomes destructive of these ends, it is the Right of the People to alter or to abolish it, and to institute new Government, laying its foundation on such principles and organizing its powers in such form, as to them shall seem most likely to effect their Safety and Happiness.

Happiness is at America's core. The purpose of our government is to secure the rights of life, liberty, and the pursuit of happiness. That government should be founded on principles that are most likely to create happiness. At the end of it all, that is why your vote matters. That is why you center on eternal truth. That is why look for a candidate that lives up to your standards. The role of government is to give you room to pursue happiness.

For voting, Commandment 10 will take you through five precepts:

1. Happiness is infinite.
2. Happiness comes from agency paired with righteousness.
3. "Privilege" is a principle of oppression.
4. Socialism is inherently covetous.
5. Build your own happiness.

By the end of your study of Commandment 10, you will be able to Proclaim, "How do you allow unfettered happiness?" We encourage you to focus on this as you study for yourself, as well as ask it of the candidates you are considering voting for.

How do you allow unfettered happiness?

Thomas Jefferson

The care of human life and **happiness**, and not their destruction, is the first and only **object** of good **government**.

Happiness is infinite

Prepare

There is no limit to the amount of happiness that the world can experience. Happiness is not a well that slowly dries-up; it is a fountain that keeps giving forever. One person's happiness does not take away from someone else's happiness. Covetousness, jealousy, comparison, etc. is contrary to happiness.

No matter how much happiness you, personally, are experiencing, you can always experience more. If you are experiencing the greatest day of your life and the most joy you have ever felt, you can still have more. If you are in the depths of despair and it feels like there's no way out, hold on. You can, and will, be happy again. That is an eternal truth. Happiness is limitless and eternal. Center yourself on eternal truth, and you will find it.

The greater part of our happiness or misery depends on our dispositions and not on our circumstances. We carry the seeds of the one or the other about with us in our minds wherever we go.

Martha Washington

I, not events, have the power to make me happy or unhappy today. I can choose which it shall be. Yesterday is dead, tomorrow hasn't arrived yet. I have just one day, today, and I'm going to be happy in it.

Groucho Marx

Ponder

Ponder

What makes you happy?

If you have more to say, additional space is available at the back of the book.

Happiness comes from agency paired with righteousness

Prepare

Agency is the ability to make choices. When you have agency, you understand right and wrong, you understand the possibilities before you, and you act accordingly. The more agency you have, the more opportunity you have to grow. Happiness is a principle of agency. When you want to be happy, you exercise your ability to make choices. Those choices lead you to different results. Good choices, moral choices, proper choices, lead you to good results. Poor choices lead to bad results. You reap what you sow. Agency paired with righteousness is the recipe for ultimate happiness.

God (with a capital "G") is the great agent. When He speaks, it is so. When we are established in eternal truth, we are more able to make choices, and choose a life that allows more happiness. God has given you the power to choose what your life will be.

 Agency is a divine gift to you. You are free to choose what you will be and what you will do.

Russell M. Nelson

Servitude, bondage, persecution, tyranny, etc. are antithetical to agency, and, therefore, antithetical to happiness. The reason centering yourself on eternal truth is so important is because the decisions you make have consequences. Addiction, debt, abuse, anger, trauma, etc. are forms of persecution and bondage. The choices you make affect both you and others. When you make righteous choices, you allow the greatest opportunity for agency (and therefore happiness), both for you and the people around you.

This is also why your candidates must be clearly centered on eternal truth. Governments can be the cause of great persecution and tyranny. The government should not have power that you have not willingly given to them. The Constitution has clearly illustrated powers for the federal government. If it tries to overstep those bounds, it is your job to hold them accountable. Your agency is yours to give, not theirs to take. Choose the government officials that give you the greatest ability to direct your life in the path you want.

Happiness is a choice, not a result. Nothing will make you happy until you **choose** to be **happy**.

Ralph Marston

Ponder

Ponder

Why does a greater ability to act make you happier?

If you have more to say, additional space is available at the back of the book.

"Privilege" is a principle of oppression

Prepare

As soon as you say that someone else has "privilege," you are allowing that to infringe on your own happiness. "Privilege," in Webster's dictionary, is defined as, "not subject to the usual rules or penalties because of some special circumstance." That's as opposed to American values as you can be. Our most core belief is that "all men are created equal." We believe in equal rights, with liberty and justice for all. In America, no one is greater or less than, even in government. We are a government of the people, by the people, and for the people. Our representatives are there to represent us, not to be made greater than us.

The moment you accept the idea of privilege, you accept that some people are simply superior. Privilege is most often seen as a product of race and sex. "White people have more privilege." "Men have more privilege." Anyone who tries to tell you that, is trying to tell you that who you are (to go back to the Webster definition) is a penalty. Privilege means that some people are less capable of success because of race, sex, income etc. "Privilege" says that some people are simply inferior.

GUTTER ODD

Those who push privilege usually follow it up with a solution to that "inferiority." Their solution is usually some sort of handout, like money, entitlements, or welfare programs. The handout is always offered by some group in a position of power. They say, "let us give you some of our privilege and superiority." Then they seek to give you a handout, and make you dependent on their services. They set themselves as superior and use these handouts to keep others "in their place," keep them dependent.

We must reject that notion. Your race, your sex, your income level, your past experiences, your nationality, your parentage, etc cannot make you lesser. You do not need handouts to be successful. You do not need someone else to define your capabilities and potential. You are a child of God. Capable of understanding eternal truth. You are eternally and infinitely valuable and capable. You are a purveyor of eternal truth. Nothing can lessen that.

As soon as you "cannot" because of "privilege," you are losing agency. You are losing happiness. Unshackle yourself of the concept that you are less than. Someone else will always have more wealth. Someone else will always have more status. Someone else will always have more power. Remember that those are man-made gods. Those are gods that do not lead to true happiness.

COMMANDMENT 10

[Remove] the bigotry of low expectations... Americans [need] an **EQUAL** chance to be rewarded for their hard work. Race should never be a factor in deciding whether or not you are qualified for anything.

Candace Owens

When you center on eternal truth, you are always capable of happiness. Happiness and satisfaction are not something you can hand out. Happiness and satisfaction are not dependent on circumstance. They are dependent on you, on your capacity to center on eternal truth, to find meaning and purpose and drive.

> **"All animals are equal, but some animals are more equal than others.**
>
> George Orwell

Ponder

Ponder

What is keeping you from experiencing more happiness?

If you have more to say, additional space is available at the back of the book.

Socialism is inherently covetous

Prepare

Socialism centers on the idea of division and inequality. It divides the proletariat, or "working class," from the bourgeois, or "ruling class." It says that the ruling class is more capable, and, by their wealth, oppresses the working class. It sees the ruling class as having more. It covets the ruling class. Socialism uses this covetousness, this jealousy, to drive a deep divide in society.

What's more, socialists try to define what happiness looks like. It bases itself on dissolving class divide, and ensuring that everyone has the same thing. It removes that divide by eliminating choice. You cannot choose the life that you want. You are assigned a life, and are stuck in it.

You are not driven to succeed by your own motivations. You are not driven by your own desires and hopes. At best, you are driven by a contrived happiness that is defined for you. At its worst (and the way it always plays out) you are driven to succeed by threat of punishment from the government.

> Socialism cannot work except through an all-powerful state. The state has to be supreme in everything. When individuals begin to exert their God-given rights, the state has to suppress that freedom.
>
> Ezra Taft Benson

Socialism defines happiness as a product of class and material goods. It defines who is better and who is worse. It seeks happiness in equalizing wealth. It takes away from those who are defined as "greater than" by their material goods and gives to those who are defined as "less than."

The grand irony of socialism is that it cannot actually work in the real world. To eliminate the classes and make the world equal, you have to have someone or a group of someones define what happiness is. You have to have a ruler, a dictator really. Socialism always leads to corruption. It always has, and always will. It must be enforced by violence because it removes motivation. It always leads to a miserable population because it removes the ingredients for happiness. It usually gives way to genocide, racism, mass crime, and, often war. It is, in every way, antithetical to happiness and eternal truth.

Ideas so good they have to be MANDATORY

It should never be forgotten that **Socialism** is always and everywhere an **impoverishing** phenomenon that has **failed** in all countries where it's been tried out. It's been a failure economically, socially, culturally and it also **murdered** over **100 million** human beings.

Javier Milei

180

The only way to overcome the "inequality" that socialism touts is to recognize that happiness does not come from "equality." The cry "all men are created equal" is really saying, "all are equally capable of happiness. All are equally valuable in eternity." Socialism does not believe in eternity; it does not believe in eternal truth; it does not see happiness as attainable in any circumstance.

> "
> When people are desperate or wealthy, they turn to **Socialism**; only when they have no other alternative do they embrace the free market. After all, lies about guaranteed security are far **more seductive than** lectures about **personal responsibility**.
>
> Ben Shapiro

Ponder

Are you a Socialist?

Ponder

If you have more to say, additional space is available at the back of the book.

Build your own happiness

COMMANDMENT

10

Prepare

You are the agent of your life. You are the steward of your destiny. Your emotions, your experiences, your whole self is yours to do with as you please. Use that wisely. Your actions have consequences, for good and bad. Build your life to be what you want. Make decisions that will lead to your happiness. Not in a fleeting sense, but in a real, eternal, lasting sense.

Your happiness is yours. Yours to define, and yours to find.

To be clear, we are not saying "just be happy." We are saying that you can build a life that makes you happy. The core of the American dream is the chance to work toward and find happiness, no matter who you are. It takes work, but you can be happy.

> **" Happiness is an inside job. Don't assign anyone else that much power over your life.**
>
> Mandy Hale

We also recognize that there are people who are experiencing mental health challenges, trauma, abuse, disease, loss, and other serious and life-altering circumstances. We affirm that you are equally capable of happiness. It may feel different than you imagine, and it will certainly take work and guidance to find, but your circumstances do not make you less capable of happiness, hope, and satisfaction. You are a miracle. You are strong, even if you don't feel like it. Hold fast to the belief that joy is yours to attain.

today I CHOOSE joy

Happiness is different for everyone. You may be happy as a grand leader who is always in the public eye, under constant scrutiny, but with great influence. You may be happy as a person who works a 9-5, and makes enough to support a good family. You may build lasting friendships by watching the game every weekend and having a beer. Maybe you find happiness working 20 hours a week, and playing video games the rest of the time. Maybe you gave up three hours of sleep to make a casserole for a family whose mother just gave birth, and you're proud to be tired the next day. Find what makes you happy. Find what drives you.

The Constitution only guarantees you the right to pursue happiness. You have to catch it yourself.

Benjamin Franklin

We are promised the right to life, liberty, and the pursuit of happiness. Happiness, in and of itself, is not a right. The opportunity to pursue happiness is a right. With that right comes the responsibility to actually pursue. When you center on eternal truth, when you know your god and know your god is good, you will find your pursuit. You will be guided to happiness.

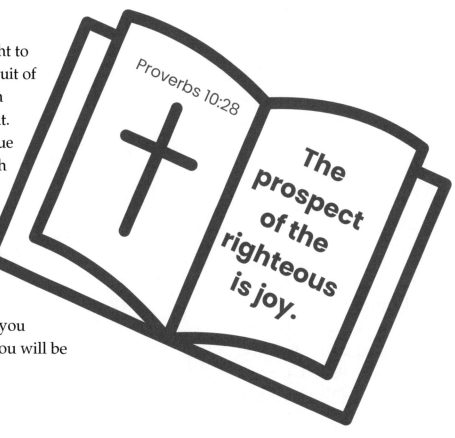

Proverbs 10:28

The prospect of the righteous is joy.

COMMANDMENT 10

Ponder

Ponder

What type of life would make you the happiest?

If you have more to say, additional space is available at the back of the book.

Proclaim your beliefs about Commandment 10 and voting

C
O
M
M
A
N
D
M
E
N
T

10

Lets look back at what you have written as you studied Commandment Ten.

As you studied, you may have written paragraphs upon paragraphs, a few words, or nothing at all. Whatever you wrote is completely fine. However, right now, we invite you to truly take a moment and proclaim in writing:

How do you allow unfettered happiness?

Put as much or as little as you like, but put something. Put something that you can say honestly, shamelessly even. It may even be aspirational. That's great! There may be something that you write

down that you feel you need to change. That's great too! This is a time to reflect as well as proclaim. Let this be something that guides you.

Then take a few more minutes to ponder any upcoming elections. With the candidates involved, what type of life do they say will allow unfettered happiness?

Take an honest look. Don't just put down what you want to be true because your emotions about it are heightened or because they are from your political party. Truly and honestly, how do your candidates allow unfettered happiness?

185

How do I allow unfettered happiness?

Proclaim

Proclaim

COMMANDMENT

10

If you have more to say, additional space is available at the back of the book.

How do my candidates allow unfettered happiness?

Proclaim

Proclaim

COMMANDMENT 10

187

If you have more to say, additional space is available at the back of the book.

Now compare.
How do the candidates match up with your own personal views?
Where are they the same? Where are they different?

COMMANDMENT 10

My happiness

My candidates' happiness

Same

Same

Different

Different

If you have more to say, additional space is available at the back of the book.

Conclusion

This has been *The Ten Commandments and Voting*. You have learned 10 Principles, studied dozens of Precepts, made 10 Proclamations, and learned how to better center your life on eternal truth. The focus of this study has been to apply the Ten Commandments to voting. You have used the Ten Commandments to measure your personal values against potential candidates. You have, hopefully, learned what you want and don't want, in a candidate, in your nation, and in your own life.

You are encouraged, now, to take this study to the next level. Whatever that means for you is fantastic, but take this further. As a starting point, go vote. There are almost non-stop elections occurring in this nation. At a local, state, and federal level, you can vote all the time. Remember, state and local elections will, likely, have the most impact over your immediate life. State and local governance will always hold more sway over your community than the federal government, so start locally.

189

In fact, start inward.

Take these teachings to the next level by taking them inward. Internalize the Ten Commandments. This program guided you through voting, but what about other aspects of your life. What about your family? Your education? Your job and career? Your relationships? Your own character?

If you really want to take these teachings to the next level, start with yourself. Find things that you can improve in your life, and improve them. Who/what are your your gods? What are the images they point you to? What do you call them? What names do you call yourself? Do you set aside time for voting? Do understand American government? Do you value life? What are your family values? How is your budget? Do you act with integrity? Do you treat others with

respect? How do you pursue happiness? You have answered these and other hard questions. While these were for voting, let these carry you forward. Let your answers change your life for the better. Don't expect immediate change, and don't expect comfort. Improvement takes time. It's an arduous and wonderful process that takes work and patience. Then once you've turned inward. Turn outward and serve. Help others. Make the world better. The surest wave to improve the nation is to start at home. Start with yourself.

The fruits of your efforts will be magnificent.

So, in the immortal words of comedian George Carlin. "Take care of yourself! Take care of yourself and then take care of somebody else!"

I have more
to say

I have more to say

I have more to say

I have more to say

I have more to say

I have more to say

I have more to say

I have more to say

I have more to say

I have more
to say

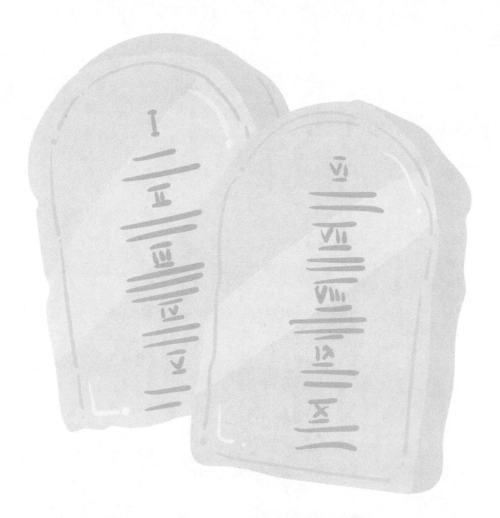

The Ten Commandments and Voting

MomSquad

momsquad.com

MomSquad

momsquad.com

Made in the USA
Columbia, SC
16 October 2024